Bullying in the Workplace

Dedication

To Chris (my other half) for his forbearance, patience, support and skill in translating my ideas onto paper.

To Frances for her diligence and perspective.

To my clients for their fortitude and belief in themselves.

Bullying in the Workplace

An Organizational Toolkit

Elaine Douglas

Gower

© Elaine Douglas 2001

The materials that appear in this book, other than those quoted from prior sources, may be reproduced for education/training activities. There is no requirement to obtain special permission for such uses.

This permission statement is limited to reproduction of materials for educational or training events. Systematic or large-scale reproduction or distribution – or inclusion of items in publication for sale – may be carried out only with prior written permission from the publisher.

Published by
Gower Publishing Limited
Gower House
Croft Road
Aldershot
Hampshire GU11 3HR
England

Gower Publishing Company
131 Main Street
Burlington VT 05401–5600 USA

Elaine Douglas has asserted her right under the Copyright, Designs and Patents Act 1988 to be identified as the author of this work.

British Library Cataloguing in Publication Data
Douglas, Elaine
　Bullying in the workplace : an organizational toolkit
　1. Bullying in the workplace – Prevention – Handbooks,
　manuals, etc.
　I. Title
　658.3'8

ISBN 0 566 08275 6 Looseleaf
　　　 0 566 08408 2 Hardback

Typeset in 11 point Plantin Light by Bournemouth Colour Press, Parkstone and printed in Great Britain by Bookcraft Ltd, Midsomer Norton.

Contents

List of figures and tables   vii

How to use this resource   ix

Part I The Manual   1

   Introduction to Part I   3

   1 Why people bully and how to understand the problem   11

   2 Putting together an anti-bullying policy   23

   3 A management system for implementing an anti-bullying policy   37

   4 Guidance for managers and HR professionals   43

   5 Guidance for individuals   57

Part II The Toolkit   67

   Introduction to Part II   69

   The toolkit matrix   70

   6 Models of behaviour   73

      Tool 1: Basic behaviour model (ABC)   74

      Tool 2: Cognitive behaviour model   76

      Tool 3: Transactional analysis model   81

      Tool 4: OK Corral model   87

      Tool 5: PUCA model   90

   7 Understanding behaviour   93

      Tool 6: Handling aggression and confrontational situations questionnaire   94

Tool 7: Locus of control questionnaire	103
Tool 8: Analyse your behaviour questionnaire	113
Tool 9: Organizational bullying questionnaire	121
Tool 10: Staff survey on bullying	127
8 Dealing with behaviour	**135**
Tool 11: Scripting	136
Tool 12: Rehearsal	139
Tool 13: Broken record	141
Tool 14: Saying 'no'	144
Tool 15: Active listening	146
Tool 16: Anger reduction	148
Tool 17: Challenging and changing thinking	151
Tool 18: Confidence boosters	156
Tool 19: Harnessing emotional intelligence	160
Tool 20: Making an action plan	172
Tool 21: Relaxation techniques	177
Tool 22: Making a buddy	180
Further reading and useful contacts	183

List of figures and tables

FIGURES

4.1	SMART objectives	52
6.1	Basic behaviour model	74
6.2	ABC model	74
6.3	Cognitive behaviour model	77
6.4	Cognitive behaviour model – sub model A	78
6.5	Cognitive behaviour model – sub model B	78
6.6	Transactional analysis ego states	81
6.7	Transactions between Adults	83
6.8	Transactions between Natural Child and Nurturing Parent	84
6.9	Transactions between Critical Parent and Critical Parent	84
6.10	PUCA model – the two continuums	90
6.11	PUCA model	91
8.1	Belief systems	151

TABLES

4.1	Pros and cons of 360 degree appraisals	50
5.1	Examples of tactics used by a bully	62
8.1	Behavioural diary – example 1	164
8.2	Behavioural diary – example 2	164
8.3	Example 1 – revised	165
8.4	Example 2 – revised	165

How to use this resource

This book is designed for anyone who wants to tackle the issue of bullying at work. It will be of particular interest to human resource and personnel professionals, but will also help anyone in a managerial or supervisory capacity. It will also give individuals guidance as to how to deal with the problem themselves if they prefer.

This book is divided into two parts. Part I (the manual) is divided into five chapters, which are intended to 'stand alone'. However, it is advisable to read Chapter 1 (Why people bully and how to understand the problem) before trying to work with individuals.

The manual will provide insight and awareness into your own (or your staff's) behaviour. From this you will be able to understand how and why people react to situations as they do. It will address both theoretical and practical issues. For example, it will provide not only an understanding of the problem, but also will put together a workable system that can be used within an organization to minimize the risk of bullying occurring, as well as specific techniques for managers and individuals. The manual will enable you to set up an anti-bullying policy within your organization, and ensure that it operates smoothly and effectively. It will help managers to identify the problem(s) and work with their staff to sort them out. Chapter 5 (Guidance for individuals) is particularly useful if you are an individual being bullied, or are seeing it happen to others.

Part II (the toolkit) contains the tools you will need to provide support to others, or to deal with the problem yourself. These surveys, questionnaires and exercises can be photocopied for ease of use. The toolkit is designed as a resource to dip into to help you to combat bullying. Each of the tools will state clearly how they can be used, in what circumstances and what you will be able to achieve.

The purpose of this manual and toolkit is to explain exactly what bullying is and why it happens, how to recognize it and what to do to combat it at an organizational and a personal level.

It would be helpful if this manual/toolkit were to be made available, either in its entirety or at least in appropriate sections, to all staff within the organization. This could be done by setting up a resource bank where employees can access journals and books discreetly for their own use.

Part I
The Manual

Introduction to Part I

Most people when they think of the word 'bullying' conjure up an image of playground thugs picking on the weak or vulnerable and those who are in some way different from them. However, sadly there is mounting evidence to suggest that bullying is not confined exclusively to a child's world, it also happens at work to adults. Although it can be physical in nature, in the workplace it is more likely to take the form of verbal or psychological abuse. Moreover, those who are targeted are unlikely to be the poorest performers or inadequate individuals. It is often the popular, enthusiastic and well-motivated workers who are good at their jobs that are singled out. Their tormentors come in many guises, but there are commonalities and patterns of behaviour that appear consistently, over prolonged periods of time.

This introduction will explain what bullying is, providing a number of definitions; consider how prevalent bullying in the workplace has become; and examine the implications of workplace bullying in terms of financial and psychological costs.

WHAT IS BULLYING?

Some researchers prefer to use the term 'psychological harassment' rather than bullying when it is applied to the workplace. There are a number of definitions:

> '... the unjust exercise of power of one individual over another by use of means intended to humiliate, frighten, denigrate or injure the victim.'
> (Workplace Bullying: Report of an NASUWT Survey of Members, 1995)

> '... persistent, offensive, abusive, intimidating, malicious or insulting behaviour, abuse of power or unfair penal sanctions, which makes the recipient feel upset, threatened, humiliated or vulnerable, which undermines their self-confidence and which may cause them to suffer stress.'
> (Bullying at Work: How to Tackle it – A Guide for MSF Representatives and Members, 1995)

> 'Bullying occurs when one person, typically (but not necessarily) in a position of power, authority, trust, responsibility, etc., feels threatened by another person, usually (but not always) a subordinate who is displaying qualities of ability, popularity, knowledge, skill, strength, drive, determination, tenacity, success, etc. The bully has conditioned himself, or allowed himself to be conditioned to believe that he can never have these qualities which he sees readily in others.'
> (Bully in Sight – Tim Field, 1996)

> 'Workplace bullying constitutes unwanted, offensive, humiliating, undermining behaviour towards an individual or groups of employees. Such persistently malicious attacks on personal

or professional performance are typically unpredictable, irrational and often unfair. This abuse of power or position can cause such chronic stress and anxiety that people gradually lose belief in themselves, suffering physical ill health and mental distress as a result.'
(Statement in the House of Lords, March 1996, reported by The Suzy Lamplugh Trust)

There are common threads running through each of these definitions. Bullying is:

- an issue of power
- an issue of control
- often an abuse of one's position
- unjust, unwarranted and unwelcome
- persistent over time
- extremely damaging in terms of physical and mental health to the victim.

What is not stated in these definitions, but which becomes apparent when one reads legal documents is that bullying is not an issue of intent. It does not matter whether the perpetrator intends to behave in an offensive way or not. What is relevant is how those actions and behaviours impact on the recipient. If he or she feels threatened or intimidated, or perceives and interprets the behaviour to be intimidating, it should be viewed as such.

HOW PREVALENT IS BULLYING?

Bullying in the workplace has probably existed for hundreds of years. The medieval serf working the land would more likely as not have been bullied and harassed by his liege lord, probably with more physical assaults thrown in than we would expect to happen these days. However, we supposedly live in more enlightened times and might naively expect that people are treated with respect and consideration. Unfortunately, it would seem that this is not the case. The nature of bullying may have become more subtle and sophisticated in that it is rare for an employer to physically attack an employee, but the principles of power, control and abuse of position still exist and are very much a reality.

Do you remember the rhyme that you probably heard as a child?

'Sticks and stones may break my bones, but names will never hurt me.'

Don't you believe it! Words are very powerful and potentially more damaging than a physical onslaught.

In the 1990s more and more information came to light about how widespread bullying is. Surveys and questionnaires distributed to staff in many different work environments produced similar results. What is also staggering is that people took the time and trouble to respond in the first place, since collecting data from surveys for research purposes is notoriously difficult. It says something when people feel so strongly about this issue that they believe that it is important to open up about their own experiences.

The following are some facts and figures relating to recent surveys into workplace bullying.

1994   Staffordshire University Business School published a survey stating that 53 per cent of UK employees (circa 14 million) had been bullied at work.

1995   The Institute of Personnel and Development published the results of a survey which indicated that around one in eight (about three million) UK employees had been bullied at work in the last five years. Over half of those who had experienced bullying said it was commonplace in their organization, and a quarter said it had become worse in the last year.

1996   MSF survey of workplace representatives. Thirty per cent of respondents thought that bullying was a significant problem and almost as many stated it had become worse in the last five years. Seventy-two per cent said their employer had no policy for dealing with bullying.

1997   TUC Bad Boss Hotline. Five thousand calls were received in 5 days. Of these, 38 per cent concerned bullying – well ahead of other issues such as low pay (25 per cent), contracts (15 per cent) and long hours (13 per cent).

1998   Trade union health and safety representatives are increasingly reporting bullying at work, and a study by the public sector union UNISON revealed 66 per cent of members having witnessed or experienced bullying at work.

Following this survey the Trades Union Congress (TUC) launched an anti-bullying campaign in October 1998.

TUC General Secretary John Monks said:

> Lifting the lid on some of Britain's most exploitative bosses has been a long and difficult process, especially when so much of the worst workplace abuses go on behind closed doors and when so many of those exploited are forced to work in a climate of fear. Trade unions and good employers need to work together to expose exploitation at work. And that is why the TUC is launching a national campaign against one of the main complaints to the bad boss line – workplace bullying.

The campaign aimed to raise awareness of the levels of workplace bullying, offered help to those affected by it, and looked at practical ways in which unions and employers could tackle the problem effectively.

The campaign was also backed by the Public Health Minister at the time, Tessa Jowell. She told the TUC conference that bullying could have damaging long-term consequences for the health of the victims, far outlasting employment with a particular company. She also announced public funding for a new information pack to help doctors identify work-related illness and provide better treatment.

Accepting that bullying is becoming more and more of a problem in organizations raises issues as to what effect this has on the workforce. There are cost implications, not just in a financial sense, but also health and safety concerns, and psychological and physical costs to the victims.

FINANCIAL COSTS

1990s

- An estimated 5 million people have been or are bullied at work, according to figures from the TUC. The financial cost is huge, with around £4 billion lost to industry as victims take time off work.
- The Health and Safety Executive (HSE) estimates 6 million working days are lost annually to stress-related illness, with bullying seen as the major component of stress.
- 1996 Institute of Management report states that each year 270 000 working days are lost to sickness absence at a cumulative annual cost to the industry, the NHS and taxpayers of £7 billion.

(These three sources are taken from Tim Field's website <www.successunlimited.co.uk>.)

2000

- University of Manchester Institute of Science and Technology (UMIST) reports that 1 in 4 people have been bullied within the last 5 years and that bullying may contribute to a loss of as much as 18.9 million working days annually. This most recent study sampled 5300 respondents from 70 organizations and included the NHS, post/telecommunications, civil service, higher education, teaching, local authorities, manufacturing industries, hotels, 'performing arts', retailing, banking, pharmaceutical industry, voluntary organizations, police, fire and rescue services and HM prison service (*Destructive Interpersonal Conflict and Bullying at Work, UMIST 2000*).

These results seem to indicate that bullying is a problem in the workplace.

Financial costs are perhaps more easily quantifiable than the effect on people's psychological well-being, but this latter cost is no less important or significant.

How does bullying affect the health and psychological well-being of the individual?

It is not always easy to make a straightforward connection between cause (bullying) and effect (ill health, poor psychological well-being). Some outcomes are more obvious than others, for example stress-related problems can often be traced back to bullying episodes. In addition to stress, there are other implications and outcomes which are perhaps not as obvious. Let's look at these further.

STRESS

People suffer from stress when they perceive that they are being threatened or placed under too much pressure. Reactions to threat and pressure vary from person to person, depending on their life experiences, temperament and effective coping strategies. However, if we concentrate on the issue of bullying and the common behaviours which have been identified, for example abuse of power and position control, it is easy to see how over a prolonged period of time someone might be badly affected.

Individuals who suffer from stress can exhibit a number of symptoms. These may include some or a number of the following:

- anxiety
- depression
- poor sleep
- fatigue
- irritability
- frequent illness (through a vulnerable immune system)
- poor concentration
- poor memory
- suspect decision-making capabilities
- shattered confidence and low self-esteem.

Stress can, therefore, be extremely damaging to a person's physical and psychological well-being.

LOSS OF CAREER AND LIVELIHOOD

When someone is being systematically and persistently bullied, they may reach a point where the situation becomes intolerable. They may feel they have no other course of action open to them other than to move to a different department or leave the company. In some cases it's a question of 'out of the frying pan into the fire', especially if the new job doesn't have the same status or prospects. Many individuals take a sideways move into another department, or even take on a job with less responsibility and challenge because they are exhausted, demoralized and their confidence is shot to pieces. However, the move may not turn out to be what they had hoped for, and bitterness and resentment creep in at the injustice of being forced out of their job.

Sometimes people leave their employment without any alternative job to go to, or opt for early retirement, neither of which is always satisfactory. Similarly, many are forced into retirement through ill health. The following extracts taken from 'No Place to Hide – Confronting Workplace Bullies', published by the National Association of Schoolmasters and Union of Women Teachers (NASUWT), illustrate these points.

> 'A sexual relationship refused, promotion within the school (or into another school) was barred. The Head left the school on an "amicable agreement" and now leads a team of OFSTED inspectors! My health suffered and after one year's absence through illness I was granted early retirement.'
> *(Female teacher bullied by Head in an independent school)*

> 'I am the fifth person to be made ill through stress in two years at this school. Now I am chronically ill and my chances of a full recovery are practically nil.'
> *(Male secondary school teacher bullied by female Head of Department)*

> 'As a result of intimidation and use of competency procedures I relinquished the role of Deputy and moved schools.'
> *(Deputy Head in grant-maintained school)*

> 'Retiring four years earlier than I had planned meant a loss of income, home improvements had to cease and private ambitions relinquished.'
> *(Author unknown)*

The NASUWT survey reported that one in five victims left their job in order to escape from their bully, and a further one in ten relinquished posts of responsibility. Medical retirements are not only confined to the teaching profession. In the year 1996–97 it was estimated that medical retirements from Britain's police force cost the taxpayer £330 million. Disillusionment and bad management were cited as primary causes; but perhaps it needs to be asked why the police officers became disillusioned, and what form the 'bad management' took.

It is not always easy to pursue redress through the courts. Legal action is expensive and because there is no specific legislation which focuses on bullying *per se*, actions are not always successful.

OTHER CONSIDERATIONS

There are other issues that could be attributed to a bullying culture in Britain.

Britain has the highest divorce rate and the highest rate of depression in adult males in Europe. We also have extremely high levels of sickness absence, stress breakdown, ill health retirement, applications to employment tribunals, suicide among adults and children, football hooliganism and road rage. Tim Field, who has undertaken a massive amount of research into bullying in the workplace, suggests that maybe we should look at all these factors and consider why our society appears to be in such a bad way. When the big picture is examined it certainly does not appear to be a healthy situation.

HEALTH AND SAFETY ISSUES

It may seem from some of the examples quoted earlier in this introduction, that employers were conspicuous by their absence. Although it may not be in evidence, employers do have a duty of care under the 1974 Health and Safety at Work Act. They have a legal obligation to ensure both the physical and the psychological well-being of their employees. Every employee is entitled to a written contract of employment which states what both the employer and employee expect of one another. The contract is valid only while both parties behave in a trustworthy manner – this is the 'implied term'. Bullying is a breach of this implied term of mutual trust and confidence.

Neglect of 'duty of care' on the part of the employer can lead to litigation. For example, in a recent case reported in *The Times* (October 1997), a trainee solicitor had complained of 'relentless sexual harassment' at work. Much of what had happened had been witnessed by a senior partner, who had taken no action. The trainee had eventually gone on sick leave as a result of this behaviour towards her, suffering from nervous debility. She reached an out of court settlement with her employer of £50 000.

In September 1998 a former chief personnel officer with the Borough of Hackney, London was awarded £750 000 compensation for years of discrimination by the former Director of Housing.

More recently, in January 2000, the warden of a travellers' camp site was awarded £203 000 for the stress he suffered as a result of being abused and bullied by his clients. His former employer, Worcestershire County Council, did not contest the case.

There have been a number of cases involving public sector employees in the fire service, police, teaching and local government. Many settlements run into hundreds of thousands of pounds of taxpayers' and ratepayers' money. Whether the money comes out of public or private funds, the trend for litigation is escalating.

LEGAL REDRESS

Litigation is costly for all parties concerned, and despite there being a number of Acts of Parliament in place to protect the employee, outcomes are not always satisfactory. The UK National Workplace Bullying Advice Line suggests that from 2000 cases of bullying, only about one in ten make it to court, and of these only about one in five succeed. This gives a success rate of about two per cent.

Grievance procedures can cost an employer at least £1000 for each of the three stages involved (that is, preparation, meeting and adjudication), and employment tribunals will cost in excess of £10 000 per stage. Proceedings may last over several days, but due to adjournments can spread over one or two years. If the situation is taken further the costs become phenomenal:

- County Court – costs at least £50 000 taking about 3 years to be heard.
- High Court – costs at least £100 000 and usually takes 5 years to be heard.
- Appeal to the House of Lords – will cost over £100 000 and usually takes 2 years for case to be heard.
- European Court – costs over £1 000 000 and usually takes 5 years.

Employers may prefer to settle out of court because of costs and the accompanying bad publicity which does their reputation little good. However, how much better it would be to adopt a preventative approach, have solid anti-bullying policies in place and effective support for employees to deal with the situation more effectively and handle themselves better.

There is no legislation which deals with bullying *per se*, and often lawyers need to look carefully at the facts of the case to find 'best fit' to current UK and EC law. The Sex Discrimination Act 1975 and Race Relations Act 1976 cover bullying and harassment when it is of a sexual or racial nature, but other legislation is open to interpretation and lacks clarity.

The Disability Discrimination Act which came into force in 1996 looks promising. Bullying or harassment of an individual classified as a 'disabled person' in accordance with the provisions of the Act will be deemed unlawful. A disability can be classified as physical or psychiatric, and the diagnosis of post traumatic stress disorder caused by bullying seems to be a possible avenue for investigation into claims against employers.

The Protection from Harassment Act 1997 was originally designed to deal with stalkers, and it has not as yet been used by an individual making a complaint against a fellow employee or an employer. However, there is potential, especially if an individual is being harassed, for example through phone calls at home when they are on annual leave or sick leave. This could particularly be the case if the calls are made during unsocial hours. Breach of confidentiality and denial of representation at meetings could also be deemed harassment.

The Employment Rights Act 1996 deals with unfair or constructive dismissal and there are other options, for example personal injury, breach of contract, common assault, breach of human rights, defamation of character, libel and slander which may be appropriate legislation to use.

SUMMARY

Research indicates that workplace bullying is a real problem and one of which we are made increasingly aware. Financial costs are phenomenal, not just in the number of working hours lost through ill health and stress, but increasingly in the awards given to individuals who pursue their case through the courts.

Psychological and physical costs to individuals are also high. People may be forced into less demanding jobs, lose status, feel they have to take early retirement, and at the same time suffer ill health both physically and mentally.

Companies themselves suffer if bullying is not eradicated. There are costs of covering for absent staff, recruiting new staff and the perhaps less obvious repercussions of reduced efficiency from the remaining workforce, not to mention the possibility of acquiring a 'suspect' reputation.

Chapter 1
Why people bully and how to understand the problem

Many people equate bullying behaviour to strong management – it isn't. Strong management is about being able to lead and manage people in a way which does not demean them but which guides, encourages, supports and directs. It is about having the ability to make tough decisions which may be unpopular, but nevertheless necessary. It is about not shrinking from responsibilities whether they are difficult or not, and it is about having the confidence, courage and ability to do the job.

Bullying is none of these things, and has nothing whatsoever to do with the concept of management. Tim Field puts it succinctly:

> 'Bullying has nothing to do with management; it is about gratification of the individual by projecting weakness, failings and shortcomings onto others as a way of avoiding having to face up to, tackle and overcome faults in oneself.'
> (Tim Field – 'Bully in Sight')

In addition to the misconception that bullying is the same as strong management, come a host of excuses which bullies trot out to try and justify their behaviour. It must be emphasized that none of these are valid explanations of bullying behaviour, and must be seen for what they are – attempts to wriggle out of situations and/or deflect the blame. Many of these phrases will be all too familiar.

> 'Only weak and inadequate people are bullied.'

Wrong. It may be the case that the playground bully singles out the child who is weaker than the others or is in some way different, but this is not necessarily the case in the workplace. Two of the most common criteria for attracting the attentions of a bully are being good at one's job and popular with people. Remember that bullies project their own failings and weaknesses onto others, so the above statement is in fact a confession of their own inadequacies.

> 'People respect toughness.'

Indeed they do. They respect individuals who show excellent leadership qualities, who can be firm but fair, loyal and trustworthy. However, bullying is not a representation of these qualities. Bullies deliberately hurt others to gratify their own needs.

'You're too sensitive.' 'You take things too personally.'

Both of the above statements demonstrate the insensitivity and prejudice of the bully. There is also denial of the consequences their behaviour has on others.

'You're over-reacting.'

No one would feel that an individual was 'over-reacting' if they went to casualty after being beaten up or mugged. It would be a normal and sensitive course of action to get checked out and know the extent of their injuries. When someone is psychologically assaulted, as with bullying, there are no visible outward signs, and yet the damage is there. Why should it not be reasonable to react to bullying in the same way as a physical attack?

'It's just a personality clash.'

In some ways there is a grain of truth in this, which makes it a very powerful excuse, and one which is often given to explain the confrontations which can occur. Thinking about this logically, however, it is not 'personality' which causes the clash, it is the behaviour which someone exhibits. In other words, someone may have a particular personality trait, say for example they are rather quick tempered by nature. This does not mean that they have to demonstrate this trait. They have choices and may choose to lose their temper or not as the case may be. This will of course depend on a number of other factors and variables, but we all have free will and are responsible for our own actions.

If someone is behaving in an unacceptable way and using bullying tactics of whatever sort, it should not be excused or dismissed.

TYPES OF BULLYING

Bullying in the workplace is often subtle and covert, as well as aggressive and overt, and it can take many forms.

Pressure bullying

Everyone has times when they are under pressure. There are often deadlines to meet, a rushed job that has to be done, or indeed volumes of work that often leave us reeling. Under these circumstances, and especially if we are tired, it's the end of the week or we are in need of a break, anyone can succumb to bullying type behaviours. Tempers become frayed and things can become tense and unpleasant.

However, it is important to recognize that this type of behaviour is usually a reaction to a set of circumstances, and should not be regarded as a problem unless it becomes prolonged.

Prolonged pressure bullying

Frequently, short-term pressure bullying becomes long-term prolonged bullying. It can happen in organizations that are reactive rather than proactive, and ones which tend to be crisis driven.

To illustrate this, there are many managers and supervisors who bully their staff into working long and exhausting hours. Whether this is because there is too much work and not enough staff to do it, or whether it is because of poor time management or fire-fighting (that is, being reactive rather than pro-active), it is hard to say unless the situation is analysed thoroughly.

In a similar vein, pressure bullying often happens as a result of poor people management skills. When junior managers are put under pressure to achieve, for example, deadlines or productivity levels, they use bullying tactics to get their staff to do what they want them to do. This is not necessarily because they are 'dyed in the wool' bullies, but because they have poor interpersonal skills, a weak grasp of the principles of managing people or have been poorly trained. It may also be the case that what they are doing is mimicking the style of their senior managers, either because they have no other strategies or because it is politic to behave in the same way as their senior managers and directors.

Organizational bullying

This type of bullying is usually a response to external pressure and is similar to pressure bullying in that unrealistic demands are placed on staff. The forces at work in this type of bullying can be changing markets, loss of market share, competition or a downturn in the economy. The organization's response to these pressures is the stick (without the carrot)! It is prevalent in organizations which support (either actively or passively) a negative culture. Staff soon learn 'what it takes to fit in here', and behave accordingly. Morale in organizations of this type is low and quite often employees are actively looking for escape routes.

Corporate bullying

This type of environment is not just negative; it is abusive and hostile. It is evidenced by coercion, for example forcing employees to work for months at a time without leave, making staff accept short-term contracts or relinquish permanent ones to save on costs and actively 'encouraging' a climate of suspicion and mistrust of fellow workers. There have been allegations recently of behaviour which would not be out of place in a Victorian schoolroom. An article in *The Daily Express* (Feb 2000) quotes from the TUC's most recent investigations an extreme example, where staff were made to stand in the corner of a room with a dunce's cap on, if their work was considered unsatisfactory. It is incredible to think that these humiliating tactics do happen.

Client bullying

This can happen to anyone who works in a client focused industry. It may be hospital workers bullied by patients and their families, teachers assaulted by students and parents, and shop assistants abused by customers. The list is endless. Sometimes this behaviour is excused under the guise of expecting better service and customers' rights. However, it is not acceptable to be harangued and abused in the name of customer service. There may also be occasions where the reverse is true, for example shopkeepers harassing customers, hotel workers their visitors, and so on. In my experience I have known professionals, who are working with vulnerable and fragile people, bullying them into opting for a particular course of action.

Serial bullying

This is a very common type of bullying and is where one individual systematically targets one victim after another and sets about making their life hell. Many years ago as a young and inexperienced teacher I can remember being bullied by the head teacher. She made my life a misery for months before moving onto the next member of staff. I can vividly remember the distress and agony this caused me, but also sadly the relief I felt when it was someone else's turn. Although this individual could not be described as having a personality disorder, in many cases there are bullies who display sociopathic tendencies.

Pair bullying

This is serial bullying carried out with a colleague. Quite often, one of the pair will be the verbal one, while the other watches and listens to what is going on. In my experience, it is the watcher who is the more dangerous of the two as they have usually been the instigator. They make the bullets for the other one to fire.

Gang bullying

This is serial bullying carried out in a group of people. This can occur anywhere, but in the type of negative or hostile environment described earlier, will be much more evident. Overt bullying – in your face – is usually how extroverts operate. In a sense they are much easier to identify because they will be vociferous and loud. Introvert bullies are much more difficult to spot as they operate 'behind your back'. They are masters at spreading rumours, dropping bits of poison here and there and generally setting people up. More often than not there will be a ringleader whom the others follow. Some of the followers will do so willingly because they enjoy the power and status they gain and the protection afforded them. Others will join because they want to ensure that they are not going to be the next victim.

Tim Field (see Further Reading) suggests that in an environment where bullying is the norm most people will either become bullies or victims. They will either join in (often as a survival tactic), or resist and therefore expose themselves to being bullied and victimized with all that implies for their own mental health and well-being.

WHAT MAKES YOU A TARGET?

Our experiences of playground bullying may lead us to believe that victims of bullies tend to be weaker individuals who appear different from the rest of us. Being vulnerable can make individuals the target of bullying, for example, being a younger member of a group of older people (or vice versa), a single parent, or living alone. Bullies will even target people who are looking after relatives or going through a difficult time emotionally, such as divorce or bereavement.

However, this is not the whole story. Many people at work are bullied because they are the antithesis of vulnerability. They are good at their jobs, popular, have high moral standards and are confident. They may also stand up for others (a sure-fire way of becoming the next victim) or find themselves unable to keep quiet about malpractice and dodgy dealings. Envy and jealousy can be strong motivators for bullies, but this is not necessarily the case. What causes individuals to bully and why they do so is quite complex and depends on a number of variables.

UNDERLYING VARIABLES

Various changes have been occurring in the workplace over the last two decades or so. This is a cause and effect analysis inasmuch that if these circumstances prevail, bullying will not necessarily occur. What it does indicate is that our changing work environment exerts certain pressures and threats, which can in turn create a climate that precipitates and even perpetuates bullying. If individuals are experiencing shifts and changes in their working lives, existing predispositions and underlying traits can become exacerbated.

The modern work environment exhibits the following trends:

1 Stress is a major factor. In modern society, security at work does not exist to the same extent as it did maybe 10 or 20 years ago. People no longer expect to be in the same job for life and uncertainty can and does cause stress. Excessive workloads and impossible demands mean that people are stretched to the limit and they may resort to behaviour which is unacceptable.

2 Changes in organizations can be difficult to cope with, especially if reorganizations take place which are unwelcome or unexpected.

3 Lack of stability is linked to insecurity. At the present time unemployment is low and the economy appears to be in good shape. However, situations can change very quickly, especially since we now have a much more global perspective, and crises further afield can and do have an effect on the UK. There is still a sense of 'not knowing what's around the corner'.

4 Understaffing is a real problem. Downsizing and re-engineering mean that staff have been laid off and not replaced. This leads to obvious increases in workload and the pressure and strain that this creates.

5 A long hours culture has become the norm. The UK has one of the longest working weeks in Europe. This leads to an impoverished quality of life. There are many working parents who do not see enough of their children, and although this may to some extent be through choice, it is not always the case. Families are suffering and again we have to consider issues of mental well-being. The irony of this insistence on long hours is that they do not necessarily equate to greater productivity and efficiency. People need a reasonable working day and the opportunity to rest. Prolonged excessive hours mean that individuals are working in overdrive, and in the end something's got to give.

6 There has been a shift towards short-term and fixed contracts. There are fewer employees on full-time permanent contracts, compared to a few years ago. This has implications for stability and security. Most working people have financial commitments, for example mortgage and rents to pay as well as emotional commitments to their families. Research indicates that children

who are uprooted regularly from school and have to move around because of their parents' jobs, have a more difficult time academically, socially and emotionally. Yet another nail in the coffin for family values.

If the overall social and economic climate is contributing to stress build-up and appears threatening and uncertain, then bullying behaviour will increase. If added to this there are some recognized psychological triggers, the picture becomes even bleaker.

PSYCHOLOGICAL TRIGGERS

As with the underlying variables outlined above, there are certain psychological triggers that for some people contribute to their behaving aggressively and directing this towards others. A distinction needs to be made here between those individuals who get angry and lose their tempers, possibly creating havoc along the way, but who can apologize and feel upset and ashamed by their actions, and those who harness their aggression in a much more destructive way.

Many individuals have quick tempers and are hot-headed. Indeed, many of them can be a pain to work with because of their volatility or unpredictability. This does not mean, however, that they are bullies. They probably need help in controlling their temper and to be made aware of the impact this has in a work setting. If they have a conscience and feel guilty about what they have done there is a better chance of enabling these types of individual to modify and change their behaviour.

The difficulty comes when aggression is channelled in a much more calculating way, where power is abused and there is deliberate intent. This is bullying behaviour, and as has been discussed it can manifest itself openly in the ridicule, embarrassment and humiliation of others; or it can be done in a devious and subversive manner which is equally damaging.

Some of the psychological triggers that can fuel anger and aggression which can lead to bullying behaviour are listed below.

Failure to achieve a goal

As individuals we often inadvertently set ourselves up to fail, and then become angry with ourselves or take it out on others when we do. This might include unrealistic goals and expectations that cannot possibly be achieved in the time frame we are given or allow ourselves. For example, is it really necessary to rewrite that letter four times when your in-tray is overflowing with things that need to be done that day? If we put pressure on ourselves to the point that we make it almost impossible to achieve our goals, we will become frustrated and angry. Most people would feel angry with themselves, but a bully will look for someone else to blame or someone to take their frustrations out on. They may even set unrealistic goals and deadlines for others which are unachievable or changed without reason or notice. Maybe part of the reason for this is the immaturity of bullies and their tendency towards peevish and childish behaviour. The unspoken message is 'If I can't get it right, I don't see why you should.'

Ambitions and wishes thwarted

We have all seen evidence of this with the red-faced toddler in the supermarket who has been denied sweets, or the vociferous adolescent who has been prevented from going to an all-night party. Someone is stopping them from having or doing what they want. Similar things happen in the workplace. Pet projects might be axed, bonuses denied or reduced, promotion prospects removed or certain cherished responsibilities passed on or shared out. In these situations bullies will plot and sabotage the efforts of others. It might be a question of 'If I can't have/do it, then I'll make sure no one else can.' They then use their power and influence to make life difficult for others, for example by reallocating work unfairly, moving the goalposts, denying leave entitlement or belittling and undermining other peoples' ideas and efforts.

Feeling threatened

If we feel threatened either physically or psychologically a primitive survival instinct kicks in. This is called the 'flight or fight' response and is triggered when we are in danger. The danger we face can be a physical one where someone threatens to attack us, or it could be a psychological threat. For example, someone may feel threatened by a young go-getting whiz kid who breezes into the office. The fear is 'Is my job threatened? Will he or she get the promotion I deserve?'

In circumstances like these there are usually two reactions. One is to run away (sensible, perhaps, if someone is trying to physically attack you) or stay and fight. The dilemma with the 'whiz kid' scenario is which to choose. Non-bullies may feel the newcomer is more able, or they may throw in the towel and concede defeat (flight). They may stand their ground and look for legitimate ways to ensure they are not overlooked (fight). On the other hand, bullies will not employ such fair-minded judgements. To cover up their own inadequacies, insecurities and most probably inferior abilities they will launch a campaign against the new colleague. This could be aimed at discrediting the newcomer or elevating themselves, or it may be a combination of the two.

The 'flight or fight' response to a real or perceived threat is perfectly normal. Self-protection is understandable, but tactics which harm or undermine the integrity of others are not self-protection, they are the tools of the bully.

Physical and mental state

Tiredness and fatigue often lead to erratic behaviour. When our mental and physical reserves are low, we do not always tackle things in an effective way. We get things out of proportion, and minor difficulties, which we would normally take in our stride, assume greater significance. We may over-react to something trivial, although we might not always be aware that this is happening. It is easy to see how pressure bullying occurs when our resources are low.

Substance abuse

It is well documented what alcohol and drugs can do to us in terms of creating chemical imbalances in the brain and altering our personality. When these are taken to excess it causes major problems. When drink or drugs are in the system individuals can behave unpredictably and, as with fatigue, can over-react or misjudge situations. The aftermath of over-indulgence is equally problematic. Usually those who work with heavy drinkers, for example, learn to avoid him or her if they have had a 'session'.

If we consider the bully it does not take too much imagination to understand how drink and drugs can make a bully's behaviour even worse. Any internal checks there are will be reduced as the debilitating properties of alcohol and drugs take effect.

OTHER REASONS WHY PEOPLE BULLY

There are many reasons why people behave badly towards others. Each individual is unique and in many ways it is an impossible task to cover all the variables at play. However, there seems to be some factors that crop up time and time again.

Personality

It has been said that some individuals are more predisposed to aggressive and difficult behaviour than others. At one time it was assumed that if children were badly behaved there was something wrong with them. Then the pendulum swung to placing the blame with the parents and possibly inadequate parenting skills. More recent thinking suggests that our personalities are shaped by both hereditary and environmental factors – in other words, nature and nurture.

A child may have a quick and volatile temper, but if his parents are easy-going and have a calming influence on him, the temper may never be as destructive as it might have been if his father and mother were of the same disposition.

Personality traits that are established in childhood can and do endure into adulthood. It is very often the case that the child bully will become the adult bully, the only difference being that the tactics may be more subtle and underhand.

Social learning theory

As we grow up we absorb the social mores, beliefs and values that are part of our family. If we were brought up in a family where there was constant bickering and fighting, we would view this as the norm and probably react in one of two ways. We would join in and behave in a similar fashion (fight) or if our temperament was less aggressive we would withdraw and not engage (flight). If we take these responses into our adult lives one can see the potential for bullies and victims. The child who is used to behaving badly and getting his or her own way will use similar tactics as an adult, whereas the child who behaves passively and is used to being terrorized will not have the wherewithal to fight back.

Similarly, for those brought up in a happy, peaceful environment, bullying tactics will be alien to them, and these people will be hurt and bewildered by such behaviour. They will not have the necessary repertoire of strategies to deal with a bully.

It is important to know that what goes on in our formative years has a very powerful effect on us as adults, although we may be unaware of its impact. If we are encouraged to be confident and independent by our parents then we will have a strong sense of self-belief. This will stand us in good stead if we do find ourselves on the receiving end of a bullying campaign. On the other hand, if we were constantly criticized or made to feel worthless as a child, or tried unsuccessfully to win the approval of a distant or uncaring parent we will not be so well grounded. Our self-esteem will be more fragile and our ability to deal with being bullied will be impaired.

The good news, however, is that we can learn to protect ourselves and overcome the negative experiences and influences that we were exposed to as children.

Causal attribution theory

Our interpretation of events governs how we will react to them. If we believe that someone is deliberately trying to hurt us, get us or put one over on us we will react more forcefully that if we feel that there is no such hidden agenda.

Here are a couple of examples:

> You are walking down the street when a youth starts running towards you. In his haste to get past you he almost knocks you over. How do you react? Would you be angry or annoyed, or possibly frightened?
> As you compose yourself you mutter something about 'ignorant kids', 'should look where they're going' and so on. However, when you look behind you the youth is holding a weeping child while her mother looks on gratefully. It transpires that the child was heading into the road, the youth spotted her and sprinted to save her. Your thought processes now would be very different from your original interpretation.
>
> You park your brand new car outside your house. Suddenly there is a loud bang. You dash out to find that your neighbour has reversed into it. What is your reaction? You are most probably extremely angry and upset. However, you discover it was an accident, her foot slipped off the brake.
> How would you feel if you believed that what she did was deliberate? She was jealous of you having a new car, so she rammed it on purpose. If you subscribe to this interpretation, the chances are you would be furious.

These examples illustrate that it is possible to misinterpret situations, to jump to conclusions and react inappropriately. Bullies tend to do this. They misjudge motives and intent – for example, believing that a junior member of staff has his sights set on their job. In so doing they 'get the wrong end of the stick' and plot ways in which they can undermine the individual. We are not necessarily talking about paranoia here, but it is not unusual for bullies to have distorted thinking about what they believe is going on.

Macho culture in organizations

Some organizations operate in a way that rewards unacceptable behaviour. For example, a high-pressure sales environment where earnings are commission based, can lead to the philosophy that it is 'every man for himself'.

People can become ruthless (especially when outcomes are directly related to their pay packet), and will ride roughshod over the feelings of others. A top salesperson may have achieved his high sales by taking away business from his colleagues, maybe denigrating them in front of clients or sabotaging their efforts. Even though he may have behaved in a thoroughly unpleasant way, he is still rewarded for bringing in the business. He gets a good income and his bosses are delighted. The message given out is that it is OK to behave like this, and the ends justify the means.

Other organizations which are very task focused risk alienating their staff if they do not pay enough attention to the process – how things get done – as well as the product. Cracking the whip and driving people to work harder, without valuing them, is a recipe for disaster, and one which is all too common. Bullying tactics may work in the short term, but in the long term they are counter productive.

Poor social skills

Some individuals have never acquired good social skills. This may be for a variety of reasons, but quite often stems back to their early years. Instead of learning interpersonal skills of give and take and negotiation, they approach situations head on and bulldoze their way through. The playground bully may well become the boardroom tyrant.

Other individuals do not read body language or non-verbal signs very well. If someone is sad or unhappy they may interpret this as being awkward or difficult and react inappropriately. They have difficulty in reading situations and lack sensibility and empathy. For example, they do not pick up on someone's discomfort or distress when telling dirty jokes or making personal or suggestive remarks. To them it is a laugh, but not to others.

Covering up for their own inadequacies

Bullies are not as confident as you might think, and their behaviour often covers up a lack of confidence in their own abilities and skills. They find it easier to intimidate and bully someone else rather than admit their own weaknesses. Have you ever heard the expression 'attack is the best form of defence'? Bullies believe it is better to get in first before someone susses out that they are not as capable as they would have everyone believe.

Bullies are often individuals who have been promoted to positions which are beyond their capabilities. This happens in organizations which use length of service as a selection criteria for advancement. Rather than admit they are out of their depth these individuals will attempt to deflect their own inadequacies onto others.

Some people have a strong need to be in control of situations and feel threatened if they have to delegate or empower others. This type of behaviour is often linked to feelings of inadequacy.

Biases and prejudice

Beliefs affect attitudes, which in turn govern behaviour. If someone believes that black people are inferior, women are weak, certain races are inherently lazy, young people are irresponsible and people from different social backgrounds are feckless or arrogant, it will affect their attitude. This in turn will lead them to behave in a certain way, possibly to the extent that these individuals are seen as fair game.

Such bigoted views can lead to extremely unpleasant behaviour. In truth, changing people's belief systems is extremely difficult, as they are often deeply ingrained. As such it is usually more effective to tackle the behaviour. This can be done by an organization adopting a policy of zero tolerance. It must be made clear that any sort of harassment, hostility or bullying which is based on racial or sexual grounds is totally unacceptable. Similarly unacceptable behaviour based on ageism, or socio-economic prejudice should not be tolerated. As stated earlier (see page 9), there is legislation in place which deals with gender and race, but unfortunately little which addresses discrimination on grounds of age or class.

SUMMARY

Bullying behaviour occurs for a number of reasons. It is useful to understand where it comes from and what triggers it. Understanding why it happens and why certain individuals may be predisposed to engaging in bullying behaviour is only the first step. If bullying is an issue in your organization you need to consider how to tackle it effectively.

Chapter 2

Putting together an anti-bullying policy

HOW WELL DOES YOUR ORGANIZATION SHAPE UP?

Answer the following questions in relation to your own organization:

- Is there a high rate of staff turnover?
- If so, is this throughout the company, or confined to a specific department or departments?
- What are the figures on sickness and absence?
- If they are high, is it the same individuals, or is there a distribution?
- Are there instances of people suffering stress breakdowns?
- Does that lead to retirement on ill-health grounds?
- Do people voluntarily seek early retirement?
- If so, is this a large percentage of the workforce?
- Is it apparent that disciplinary procedures are invoked regularly?
- Are there a number of formal complaints and grievances issued?
- Are people suspended from work?
- Are there quite a number of dismissals?
- Is there any evidence that the organization uses private security firms to snoop on its employees?
- What is the company's history with regard to employment tribunals or legal action against employers?

If you can identify with the above indicators then it is highly likely that you work for a company or organization which has a pervasive bullying culture. For a more in-depth analysis, see the questionnaire on identifying a bullying organization in Tool 9 in the toolkit. If your responses give you a score in the 'red zone', then there are some serious issues that need urgent attention. Scores in the 'amber zone' do not necessarily mean that all is well. You should be alerted to the possibility that difficulties may develop.

A POLICY FOR ORGANIZATIONS

Once the commitment is there from those in positions of control, that is, the decision-makers of the company, then it is possible to start putting together a policy to combat bullying. There are informal and formal procedures which should be set up, and ways in which all of this must be communicated to the workforce. It cannot be stressed strongly enough that for any policy to work there must be the two elements – commitment and communication. This is even more important when dealing with such an emotive issue as bullying. Many policy documents, which some poor souls have sweated over to produce, lie gathering dust on a shelf somewhere. Why is this? Usually it is because it has no relevance, or is perceived to have no relevance to the organization. If people only pay lip service to something, their motivation to make it work will be poor and their commitment half-hearted.

In order to put together a successful policy to combat workplace bullying, not only is commitment needed from the top but also involvement from the rest of the staff. Asking staff for their ideas and suggestions can be done through an internal survey (see toolkit, Tool 10), and the information gleaned can then be used to enhance the preparation of the policy document. Pulling in members of staff from across departments and at different levels within the organization to work on the production of the document will ensure a broader representation of views and opinions. There is more likely to be a feeling of corporate ownership of the policy, and with it the will and motivation to make it work.

Once the policy document is completed, the rest of the workforce needs to know exactly how it looks and what it means for them. This will not be achieved simply by issuing copies of the policy to staff. How many of us can be bothered to read something like this? We might flick through the pages, mutter 'what a good idea' or 'about time' but we will not absorb the finer points of what it is trying to achieve. Educating employees, at whatever level, is crucial. This can be done through staff seminars and workshops which take them through the process, what it means for them and what to do should they be on the receiving end of, or witness, the occurrence of bullying.

WHAT SHOULD THE POLICY CONTAIN?

The following elements are needed in any type of policy dealing with bullying:

1 Statements of the beliefs of the organization.
2 Definitions of bullying and harassment, with examples to illustrate.
3 What the effects and costs are to the organization and to the individual.
4 The legal implications.
5 The role of the manager.
6 The role of the personnel department and human resources staff.
7 The role of the employee.
8 Procedures:
   – informal
   – formal.

FRAMEWORK FOR AN ANTI-BULLYING/HARASSMENT POLICY

A policy should contain something about the organization's philosophy, definitions and examples of bullying, the legal and financial costs and implications, the roles of staff within the organization and the informal and formal procedures.

Statements of beliefs

These need to state emphatically what the organization believes in and what it intends to achieve. Some of the statements below may be of help:

- The company is opposed to any form of discrimination including harassment and bullying being practised against its employees on any grounds. (Specific grounds may include race, creed, sex, marital status, age, physical and mental disability, religious or sexual persuasion, AIDS/HIV.)
- The organization is committed to achieving genuine equality of opportunity for all its employees.
- The organization is committed to making full use of the talents and resources of all its employees. It wishes to promote a healthy working environment where all employees are given the dignity and respect to which they are entitled.
- The organization seeks to provide an environment of mutual trust and respect amongst all the workforce.

Definitions of bullying and harassment

In addition to those definitions given in the Introduction on page 3, there are some which have been used by specific companies and organizations:

> 'Harassment is defined as unreciprocated and unwelcome comments or actions which are considered objectionable by the recipient. The policy encompasses harassment with regard to gender, race, sexuality, disability, religion or age ... In addition the organization will actively promote an environment which is free from inappropriate behaviour such as bullying and intimidation.'
> (Promoting employees' dignity at work policy statement, Littlewoods, 1994)

> 'Various patterns of behaviour are considered acceptable between people as normal forms of social and business interaction, others are considered inappropriate and the recipients may feel harassed or bullied.'
> (Harassment/bullying policy, Nationwide Building Society, 1996)

Harassment and bullying can take many forms and may involve:

- inappropriate actions
- persistent offensive, abusive or intimidating behaviour
- abuse of power or unfair penal sanctions
- malicious or insulting language
- physical contact that is objectionable or causes offence
- name calling
- excluding a colleague from the team
- non-verbal conduct, for example the displaying of distasteful pictures.

Conduct which may be acceptable or tolerable to one individual, but which makes another individual feel upset, harassed or bullied may be considered to be harassment, for example where it makes an individual feel:

- upset
- humiliated
- threatened

- vulnerable
- that his or her privacy is being invaded
- that his or her self-confidence is being undermined leading to undue stress.

(Harassment/bullying policy, Nationwide Building Society, 1996)

It must be stressed that these examples are just that – examples. They are not a definitive list of bullying behaviours or emotional responses. For a thorough and comprehensive account of bullying behaviours, Tim Field's book *Bully in Sight*, is an excellent resource (see Further reading and useful contacts, page 183).

Some policy documents define very clearly what is meant by, for example, sexual harassment. You may wish to consider whether it is appropriate for your organization to go into such detail.

Again, the following definitions and statements may help.

Race

This is harassment based on race, nationality or national origins where the individual believes that he or she is being harassed on racial grounds. Examples would include racial abuse of a physical, verbal or prejudicial nature, racist jokes, insults, ridicule or name calling. It would also include racially offensive written or visual material.

Discrimination on the grounds of race could be more subtle and covert. This might include unfair allocation of work, unequal treatment in the application of conditions of employment, unreasonable pressure to complete tasks, exclusion from conversation or activities, or unreasonable withholding of permission to attend self-organized groups within the workplace or trade union.

However, it must be acknowledged that the above points can relate to all employees and not just racial minorities and different cultures. There are many behaviours which could in essence come under any of the headings of bullying, harassment and discrimination. Perhaps this is why, as we have seen, applying the relevant legislation to a particular case can be so tricky.

Gender

This is unwanted conduct of a sexual nature, or other conduct based on gender affecting the dignity of women and men at work. This would encompass physical conduct, for example unnecessary touching or invasion of personal space. It could include verbal conduct such as unwelcome propositions, suggestive remarks or innuendo. Non-verbal conduct might include the displaying of suggestive or pornographic material, leering or suggestive gestures.

Disability

This is unfair and unwelcome treatment based on the fact that an individual has a physical or sensory impairment, learning difficulties or is experiencing mental distress. It would include offensive, threatening or patronizing language, denial of that person's identity, and failure to provide facilities and resources to enable them to perform their duties.

Lesbians and homosexuals

This is harassment and discrimination based upon the belief that lesbians and gay men are inferior to heterosexuals. Some of the behaviours would be similar to those outlined under gender, but may also include intrusive questions or derogatory comments about an individual's personal and domestic circumstances.

The effects and costs

Harassment and bullying are infringements of employees' rights, but it can also affect their mental and physical health and well-being. Anxiety and stress can lead to increased absence and sickness, or even job resignations.

If bullying and harassment are ignored, or even condoned, there will be a knock-on effect within the workforce. Reduced efficiency and damaged morale may ensue. Staffing costs will increase as replacements or temps need to be found to cover for sick colleagues. Those companies who do not pull in staff to cover, but who spread the work amongst existing staff, risk exacerbating the problem.

As a number of policy documents point out, each member of staff is responsible for their own behaviour and it is their duty to be sensitive to the needs of others.

You may feel it appropriate at this stage to introduce some facts and figures (see Introduction, pages 4 and 5), although this will need to be done judiciously so as not to create undue anxiety or concern.

Legal implications

Any policy document needs to make it absolutely clear that there are legal implications to be considered if an employee feels that they are being bullied, harassed or discriminated against, and that they have the right to take their employer to court. The process may be lengthy and tortuous, but whether you agree with it or not, we are becoming a much more litigious society. What is more, cases are being won with claimants receiving substantial damages.

It is imperative that the message gets across to employers and employees that prevention is better than cure. A proactive policy will identify problems before they get to the stage of legal proceedings.

Role of the manager

Managers need to do the following to ensure that their organization supports a non-bullying culture and unacceptable behaviour is not tolerated:

- Managers need to look to their own behaviour. They must treat employees, customers and clients with dignity and respect.
- They must be aware of what is acceptable behaviour and what is not, and be alert to the signs. Since much of what goes on is not always immediately apparent as bullying, they must be particularly vigilant to some of the more covert warning signs.

- They must ensure that employees are familiar with the anti-bullying/harassment policy and know what to do.
- As new employees join the company, the policy should form an integral part of their induction training.
- Managers need to ensure that staff who make a complaint about bullying or harassment are fully supported before, during and after complaints are investigated.
- Complaints should be dealt with promptly, fairly and with total confidentiality. The rights of all parties should be respected at all times.
- Managers should be aware that it is the impact that the behaviour has on the victim or claimant which determines bullying or harassment, *not* the intent.
- Many problems in the past have been put down to 'personality clashes'. Managers must not fall into this trap and be dismissive of an allegation; they should investigate the situation thoroughly.
- Support for the complainant is vital. It is the manager's responsibility to ensure that the complainant is not victimized or retaliated against for bringing a complaint forward.
- Managers need to make sure that the policy is fully implemented.

Role of personnel/HR

Because personnel and HR departments should generally speaking be more *au fait* with 'people' issues, they are ideally placed as a resource for managers who are perhaps unsure of how to deal with staff who are emotionally upset. This does not mean that personnel staff should take over. It is the manager's responsibility to manage their department, not personnel's. However, the personnel/HR department can offer support and guidance as to how to manage the process.

Staff should also be able to contact the personnel department directly. However, there needs to be a degree of flexibility here. Members of staff will not approach someone whom they perceive as being unsympathetic or perhaps indiscreet. They will either say nothing and suffer in silence, or they will discuss it with someone whom they trust.

Role of the employee

There is a lot that employees can do to prevent harassment and bullying from taking place, for example:

- Employees need to be aware that bullying can and does happen. They should make sure they understand the issues surrounding bullying.

- They need to be aware of their own conduct and behaviour. They may unknowingly be causing offence. What they see as harmless banter or 'just a bit of fun' may be misconstrued by others. Some people will not take offence to personal remarks, sarcasm or put downs, but others will. Employees need to be absolutely sure that their own prejudices and beliefs are not interfering with how they treat others.

- If an employee is being bullied or harassed then something needs to be done, they do not have to put up with it. Before they go down the road of speaking to their manager, supervisor or whoever is appropriate, they can learn how to stand up for themselves. (Techniques on assertiveness can be found in the practical toolkit section, and Chapter 5 'Guidance for individuals' will help.)

- If an employee witnesses someone else being bullied, they can help by supporting them. Many bullies rely on the fact that people don't want to get involved. It may only be at the level of providing a shoulder to cry on, but that in itself will mean a lot to the person being bullied. It should be remembered that if a member of staff sees or hears something and does nothing, they will be seen as condoning the behaviour and colluding with the bully.

The procedure

The object of any anti-bullying policy should be to try and solve the problem as quickly as possible. However, this must be balanced alongside ensuring that the process is thorough and fair, taking into consideration the rights of all parties. Wherever possible an informal approach should be used initially. Many cases can be resolved at this stage. However, the option to choose the formal procedure should be available at any time.

Informal procedure

If someone is being treated by a colleague or manager in a way that they believe constitutes harassment or bullying, that individual should try if at all possible to deal with the problem themselves. If they are able to speak to the alleged perpetrator they should tell them that their behaviour (whatever form it takes) causes offence and they want it to stop. If the behaviour of the alleged perpetrator is aggressive or threatening they should walk away, making it clear that they do not wish to be treated in this manner.

Employees who are being bullied should keep records of what has happened, where, when and how they felt at the time and, if possible, who witnessed it. Written accounts are vital and must be done soon after the event. Memories can be selective or unreliable.

If the employee is unable to confront the individual, they may wish to write a letter. This should state the following:

- the offensive behaviour, being specific and accurate
- when, where and at what time it occurred
- why the employee objects to it
- that they want it to stop.
- how they expect to be treated in the future.

The employee must make sure they keep a copy.

If the employee is frightened or anxious (which is often the case), they may feel unable to do any of this. If this is the case they may wish to ask a work colleague, their manager or a trade union representative to make this approach on their behalf. If a conversation or meeting takes place, again make sure that an accurate record is kept.

The employee may wish to discuss the matter with someone, such as their supervisor or line manager, before they try and tackle the problem themselves. In a lot of cases, however, it is the 'boss' who is the problem, and provision must be made for the complainant to discuss problems with someone who is impartial and objective. This may be someone from the personnel or human resources department, but may be another designated person within the organization.

The employee may wish to have a work colleague, friend or union representative with them at this initial stage. This should not be discouraged if it provides support for the individual, but issues of confidentiality must be stressed to all involved.

Reassurances must be given at this stage that the individual will be protected from further harassment and bullying. Individuals need time and space to decide what course of action to take.

From an initial meeting there are a number of options available:

1. The complainant may feel confident to speak to the alleged perpetrator.
2. They may wish to do this with the support of the person they have discussed it with.
3. The designated person (for example, supervisor or personnel officer) may speak informally to the alleged offender about this particular issue.
4. The designated person may speak to the alleged offender in more general terms about bullying, pointing out that it is a disciplinary offence. They may not necessarily mention the complaint.
5. If it is feasible or appropriate, consideration may be given to rearranging desks or work allocations to reduce the risk of contact with the alleged offender.

In many instances, the person who is behaving in a manner which causes offence may be unaware that this is the case. An informal approach may well do the trick and the behaviour will stop. Even if the behaviour is more deliberate, intervention can be very successful when done informally. Sometimes it is enough that they have been confronted with the consequences of their actions. However, one needs to be mindful of the fact that the bully may become more devious in their bullying tactics, or indeed that they take no notice whatsoever and carry on as they have been doing, perhaps with more intensity. If this happens, the victim of bullying must consider seriously whether they are going to step up a gear into formal action.

For some, the prospect of invoking formal procedures can be a daunting one. It is worth remembering, though, that if the bully carries on, the problem is unlikely to go away, and may even get worse. Victims of bullying may well need a lot of support at this point.

It is worth noting that some organizations ask for volunteers to be involved in this support process. They are then trained in using counselling skills to work with the individuals and help them to regain control and improve their self-confidence.

Formal procedure

It should be possible for a formal complaint to be made at any time, although it is always useful to try the informal approach first.

All complaints of harassment or bullying should be treated seriously, and prompt action must be taken as such complaints may lead to serious disciplinary action. If a complaint is made and an investigation follows, the interests of the complainant and alleged perpetrator should be taken into consideration. Counselling should be available and offered to both parties.

Some organizations will already have a discipline and grievance procedure in place. If this is the case, a complaint is usually made in writing to the immediate boss or to an appropriate person within the company. This may be someone from the personnel department, human resources department or a designated officer.

The following guidelines are intended for those companies or organizations who do not have a formal discipline and grievance policy, but equally they will offer some pointers to those who do.

GUIDELINES FOR THE COMPLAINANT

It is usually more professional to make a complaint in writing. The complainant needs to document facts and how any incident or incidents have affected them and made them feel. Facts will include what happened and when, in what circumstances and whether there was anyone else present. The complainant should also include any discussions which might have taken place with the perpetrator, either with themselves, or others, in an attempt to sort out the problem. Dates, times and a résumé of what was said are helpful.

If the person who is accused of bullying is the complainant's immediate boss, then they must send their complaint to a senior person or to someone from the personnel department. (This information should be available in the staff handbook.)

An investigation will follow. The complainant will be interviewed by the investigating officer, and may have representation (that is, a union officer, colleague or friend) during the interview.

There will be a defined time limit on the process, and the complainant will be informed of the outcome in writing.

If they do not agree with the findings, they may appeal against the decision.

GUIDELINES FOR THE INVESTIGATING OFFICER

It is useful to hold a preliminary interview to establish that the complaint warrants further investigation. This would clarify the nature of the complaint, establish dates, times, places, names and any existing evidence.

The officer will need to explain to the complainant what is going to happen. This will include:

- the length of time taken to investigate the complaint
- an offer of counselling and support during the process
- an offer of support by a union representative or colleague
- an explanation of the interview process
- notification of the outcome and appeals procedure

- an explanation of the disciplinary options available, should the complaint be upheld
- a caution that any malevolent or malicious complaints or allegations will be treated as a disciplinary offence.

Assuming that further investigation is required, a realistic timetable needs to be set, to minimize stress to all parties. Both the complainant and alleged perpetrator should be kept informed if, for any reason, there are delays.

The complainant should be asked whether they would like any assistance during the process.

Immediate temporary action should be taken to minimize contact between the claimant and the alleged perpetrator if requested, or is considered necessary or appropriate by the manager.

It may be considered necessary to suspend either or both parties on full pay during the course of the investigation.

Interviews should take place with the complainant, the alleged perpetrator and any witnesses. These should be separate, private and confidential. They should be conducted in an objective manner without bias or prejudice to either party.

Age and gender should be taken into account. For example, a female complainant might feel uncomfortable discussing these issues with a male member of staff, especially if the alleged bully is also male. Similarly, a male may not relate well to a female investigator. If it is not possible to provide both male and female investigators, then it may be useful for the complainant to have a representative of a similar age and gender supporting them through the process.

An accurate record must be made of the investigation and the conclusions reached. Both parties should be informed in writing of the findings of the investigation and the action to be taken. Such a letter should also emphasize that any victimization or reprisals that occur as a result of the investigation will not be tolerated.

If the complaint is upheld, prompt disciplinary action in the form of a disciplinary hearing should take place. The complainant may be required to give evidence in person. However, it may be possible for a duly elected third party to represent the complainant. The decision of whether or not the complainant should attend will lie with the persons hearing the case. If the complainant is required to attend they should be allowed a supporter to accompany them. The same applies to the alleged perpetrator.

If the complaint is upheld at the disciplinary hearing, it will depend on the nature of the complaint as to what action is taken against the perpetrator. Some of the options might be as follows:

- A disciplinary warning which remains on the employee's personal file for a period of twelve months, after which, if no further complaint has been made, it will be removed.

- The offender may be given an alternative post, or work may be relocated so that he or she and the complainant do not have to work in close proximity.

- Certain behaviours may constitute gross misconduct and may result in dismissal. These may include demands for sexual favours which could affect an individual's job performance, job security or career prospects. It could also include unwelcome, intentional physical contact of a sexual nature, racial attacks, physical assault and threatening behaviour.

Each case should be examined on its own merits.

Both the complainant and the alleged perpetrator should have the right to appeal against the decision of the hearing, or against any disciplinary action taken.

GAINING COMMITMENT FROM THE TOP

If a company is to be successful in implementing a policy, the leadership and impetus must come from the top. This is not to say that it won't work if the push comes from another department (for example, the personnel department) in the first instance. However, unless those who are the most senior in the organization are committed to encouraging an environment which does not support bullies, it will be an uphill struggle. Employees need to feel that their managers are sincere and genuine in supporting an anti-bullying policy, otherwise mistrust and suspicion will take over.

If a need has been identified by a like-minded group of individuals, or indeed by one person who wants to make changes, there are things which can be done to inform and persuade the 'powers that be' that a policy is necessary.

First and foremost, it is unlikely that any senior manager is going to be swayed by arguments which rely solely on the 'touchy, feely' area of employee emotional and psychological well-being. They will be more impressed by data and factual evidence. This is where information from the questionnaires in the toolkit can prove extremely useful. This, however, is qualitative data; it is based on people's opinions and interpretations of the situation. This material needs to be backed up with a statistical analysis of sickness and absence records, turnover of staff, average length of service in the organization and, if it adds weight to the argument, turnover and percentage growth of the company. This analysis does not have to be complicated. Histograms and pie charts can give a very potent visual representation of what is going on. Added to this other quantitative data could be included, for example information on complaints that may have been made, and if exit interviews are undertaken with staff who are moving on, their reasons for doing so.

The purpose of this exercise is not to point the finger at particular individuals, more to convince those who need to be convinced that 'all is not well in the state of Denmark'! (with apologies to William Shakespeare).

Once the evidence has been marshalled it is time to consider how to put the argument across as cogently and effectively as possible. In the scenario outlined here, the best influencing strategy to use is one of persuasion. Persuasion relies on logical reasoning using the material prepared to back up the argument. With most companies the bottom line will be 'What are the costs and benefits to us as an organization?' To this end it is useful to think this through before the case is presented. Bearing in mind the old adage that 'prevention is better than cure', it is always better to prepare for any objections or concerns before they are raised during the presentation of information. Another useful technique is to try and get a feel for how people are thinking before trying to put the argument across. This is not always possible, but if it can be done it is valuable knowledge which can be helpful.

It is also useful to give people a summary of the points you are going to raise before you set up the meeting. Admittedly, 'forewarned is forearmed' and this can lead to any opposition being prepared in advance to counter your argument. However, what it does mean is that what you present in the meeting will not hold any surprises which may throw people off balance. The last thing you need is to create a situation where people feel threatened so that they have to go on the defensive.

During your meeting and presentation, try and use the facts to your advantage by securing agreement that this is not a happy state of affairs. It is hard to argue against factual data, and if this is accepted then it is more a question of offering solutions to the problem.

There are always a number of courses of action, some of which are going to be more acceptable than others. It might be helpful to ask those involved to 'brainstorm' some ideas, bearing in mind that criticism and judgement should be suspended at this stage. When ideas are exhausted it is then time to sift through and put some shape and form to the suggestions. If preferred, the presenter may wish to put forward two or three options, which can then be discussed.

Hopefully, by this time the option to do nothing will have been rejected, but if there is strong resistance agree a future meeting, say in two or three months' time. Gather as much additional evidence as you can and go through the process again. In those intervening months try and find out why there is resistance and see if it is possible to come up with a solution which allays fears and goes some way to setting up a course of action.

It is advisable to have a plan put together when meeting senior executives, even if agreement is not reached at this early stage. This does not have to be a lengthy or wordy document. However, it does need to contain the elements necessary for strategic planning, for example:

- What are your objectives?

   To set up an anti-bullying policy within the organization.

- What needs to be done to achieve your objectives?

   The plan needs to be broken down into its component parts, for example draft policy, distribution for comments, time-scale for implementation, staff training for roles and responsibilities, staff handbook, dissemination of information.

- What is needed in terms of resources to achieve your objectives?

   Resources means costs incurred for both materials and people. You will need to consider how much it will cost to produce materials, for example staff handbooks and which people will need to be trained up for specific roles, for example counsellors, investigating officers and arbiters.

Try not to be over-optimistic in terms of your time frame, remember all the other jobs and tasks that have to be done within the organization. Think about seasonal variations in work loads. However, it is a question of balance, since drawing things out over a protracted period of time means that you will lose the impetus.

If your efforts are initially unsuccessful, don't lose heart. Keep trying using rational arguments and all your persuasive, assertive skills. You will get there in the end.

STAFF HANDBOOK GUIDELINES

A brief summary of the behaviours that the organization is seeking to reduce can be put into a staff handbook, together with information as to what to do should a member of staff be the victim of bullying or an observer.

It is also quite helpful to have an introductory statement from the managing director, chairperson or chief executive of the company. This statement lets everyone know that there is commitment from the top, that is, the most senior person within the organization.

The handbook should look something like this:

1. Statement from the chairperson/MD.
2. Behaviours that the policy seeks to prevent, for example:

   - sexual harassment
   - racial harassment
   - age discrimination
   - discrimination against disabilities
   - religious discrimination
   - bullying
   - victimization.

3. What to do if you are a victim of bullying:

   - Try and deal with it yourself.
   - Ask for help. Informal advice is available from (for example):
     - nominated supporters (names and numbers should be available in the handbook or prominently displayed, for example, on a notice board)
     - the employee's supervisor or line manager
     - the personnel/HR department
     - the equal opportunities department
     - the trade union representative.

   - Employees can use a formal procedure and make a complaint using the company's grievance procedure.
     - Complaints should be addressed to the employee's immediate superior, line manager, personnel department or equal opportunities department, being aware that any malicious complaint will result in disciplinary action. Choosing to use any of these channels will not result in victimization, whatever the outcome.
     - Each complaint will be investigated thoroughly, promptly and impartially.

   - What else can employees do? They can help to put a stop to bullying and harassment by:

- being aware that it happens and what the consequences are
- setting a good example and ensuring that their own behaviour doesn't cause offence or misunderstanding
- not being afraid to make a stand against the injustice of discrimination, harassment or bullying – whether they are personally involved or are providing support for a colleague.

All members of staff from junior up to senior must have a copy. Managers should make sure that new and incoming staff are aware of the policy and what the procedures are should they witness or experience bullying or harassment.

Organizations may find it helpful to put a copy of the handbook on the company intranet. This would make it readily accessible to everyone who has access to a computer.

SUMMARY

It is well worth the time and effort involved in establishing an anti-bullying policy. If it is done thoughtfully and thoroughly it will send out a very positive message to staff. However, it is not enough on its own. A system must be put in place to manage and implement it.

Chapter 3

A management system for implementing an anti-bullying policy

Once commitment is gained and the policy document has been put together, or is well on its way, it is time to consider how it will be implemented. This means looking at briefing staff, training them, preparing counsellors, supporters and investigators, and ensuring there are sufficient resources to implement the policy. The role of the manager must be clear so that the system runs smoothly and impetus is maintained. In addition, some checks must be put in place to ensure it is working effectively.

BRIEFING STAFF

It is not sufficient to dish out the staff handbook and then assume that everyone will subscribe to its philosophy. Being committed to an anti-bullying ethos within an organization means *actively* showing that you are.

It will depend on the size of the organization as to how these briefings are carried out, and whether it is feasible to get everyone in the same place at the same time. However, this should be the goal to aim for. It will also be more effective to have the most senior members of the organization speaking to the rest of the staff. In this way they will be physically endorsing what has been written in the policy document and handbook.

These briefing sessions do not need to be long, drawn out affairs. It should be possible in 30–45 minutes to explain what the company is trying to achieve and how it intends to go about it. A briefing session will deliver a strong message to the workforce, and if everyone is gathered together at the same time, the same message will be given out to all members of staff. Those who are bullies will receive the message that unacceptable behaviour will not be tolerated, and those who are the victims will feel that there is a light at the end of the tunnel.

TRAINING STAFF

A briefing session should give an overview of why it is important to have an anti-bullying climate in an organization, but it will not go into detail as to what bullying is, how to identify it and what to do about it. This is where training comes in.

The organization may have its own training department, in which case it should have the necessary skills to put together a training programme for its staff. Other organizations may feel that they don't have the necessary expertise 'in-house' and would prefer to outsource the training to an external provider. As with any training provision there are pros and cons to using internal or external resources. Perhaps a word of caution is needed here. If it is decided to use external consultants it is far more beneficial to use those who can tailor the programme to the needs of the individual organization, rather than those who produce a blanket course that covers every eventuality. The material used in, for example, the finance sector and manufacturing industries may be very similar as the principles involved are transferable, but trainers need to understand the uniqueness of each company.

Again, how the programme is developed will depend on the organization. However, there are some points which need to be thought through which are pertinent to all organizations:

- Think through what the aims and objectives are.

- Will these be achieved and met in a course or workshop that is half a day or a day's duration?

- Does it need to be run over a longer period of time so that behaviour change can be seen?

- Where will it take place – on site or off site?

- How will the mix of staff be achieved? It might be better to have an inter-departmental cross-section, with staff of different levels rather than on a departmental basis, or doing it by grades or levels.

- How do you ensure that **all** staff go through the process? How will you overcome possible resistance? If people are resistant there may very well be a good reason. They could be bullies who do not relish the prospect of confronting and acknowledging this type of behaviour, or they may be victims of bullying who cannot face something which will trigger off their own painful memories and experiences. Resistance needs to be handled sensitively, and it should not be assumed that someone is being deliberately awkward. In any event it is important for all staff to receive training, but some individuals may need one-to-one counselling before they are ready to attend the programme.

- Think about how the course will be run. It needs to be interactive with plenty of opportunity for role play, case studies and simulation exercises.

The toolkit section of this manual is a resource that can be used in preparing a training programme.

Training may identify individual needs. It may well be that the experience is a difficult one for those who have been bullied, even if support was given prior to the training. If this happens it would be useful to offer some individual coaching in specific skills, for example, assertiveness and/or further counselling, after the training session.

PREPARING COUNSELLORS, SUPPORTERS, INVESTIGATORS AND MEDIATORS

If the organization is intent on making the policy work, it needs to ensure that any staff who have agreed to take on a specialist role are thoroughly trained. This training will be separate from, but additional to, the training given to all staff.

Counselling is often misunderstood and often much maligned. Its purpose in this context (as in any other for that matter) is to empower the individual and enable them to take control of their lives. It is not about creating dependency and helplessness. Counsellors need to be properly trained in counselling skills, and to understand when someone's difficulties are beyond the scope of their expertise. People who earn their living as counsellors and therapists learn their craft over two or three years. Obviously, one would not expect or request this level of training for staff working in a counselling capacity at work. However, they need to receive basic training in the core techniques, otherwise they may do more harm than good.

A basic course on counselling should contain training in:

- listening skills
- core elements of empathy, genuineness and respect of the individual
- learning to be non-judgemental and non-directive
- counselling theories – at the very least knowing about the work of Carl Rogers and his person-centred approach (see Further reading and useful contacts, page 183)
- specific techniques for helping people to talk things through.

A supporter may wish to be trained in basic counselling skills, but if their role is more one of a befriender, it may not be so vital. However, what is important is that they are aware of their own limitations and that they resist the temptation to assume a 'pseudo' counselling role. Victims of bullying are often vulnerable and fragile, and it is all too easy to damage them further by possibly giving advice or making suggestions which are not appropriate to their circumstances. Most people who are interested in the role of counsellor or supporter are very well meaning and want to help, but they could make matters worse if they are ignorant about the skills needed in counselling.

Those appointed to look into allegations of bullying must also be trained in basic counselling skills. They will be dealing with distressed individuals (both bullies and victims), and this requires a high level of sensitivity.

Investigators need also to be skilled in interviewing alleged victims and perpetrators. They will need to be trained in how to use constructive questioning (that is, open, closed and probing questions), and how to establish facts rather than opinions.

Organizations might want to consider offering a mediation service after the investigations have taken place. It can be particularly worthwhile if the two parties are still employed by the company, and even more so if they have to work in reasonably close proximity.

A mediator needs to be highly skilled in facilitating discussion between those involved, and this can be tricky if not handled well. The choice of staff for this role is important, as they must be someone with excellent interpersonal skills, who is impartial and objective and of a reasonably high status within the organization to have credibility. As with counsellors, supporters and investigators, they will need training in counselling skills as well as what the mediation process entails.

Additionally, they will need to be very familiar with the informal and formal processes involved in an investigation, as well as having an understanding of tribunals, legal matters and relevant statutes.

There is also an issue here about caring for the carers. In other words, looking after the staff who take on these roles. The work can be exhausting and emotionally draining and organizations need to make certain that they offer debriefing opportunities as well as clinical supervision. Clinical supervision is not the same as supervising someone in the normal work sense. It is about making sure the counsellor is working safely with their client and also that they are attending to their own needs. Some larger organizations may wish to consider setting up an occupational health department or employing a psychologist or mental health professional to act in a consultative capacity. For smaller firms this may not be a viable option, but they might want to consider some of the services provided by companies who offer employee assistance programmes (EAPs).

EAPs are becoming more and more popular as a means of tapping into professional expertise which is not available in the organization itself. Some companies offer counsellors who will see individuals on a face-to-face basis; others offer telephone counselling. There are a number of options available, which as long as they become an integral part of the company's policy towards bullying, could prove to be extremely helpful and useful.

RESOURCE IMPLICATIONS

If staff do take on the responsibility of counselling, they may need some help with fulfilling their other duties. This might be a question of sharing the work out among colleagues or even reducing some of their normal work load so that they can counsel the individual. One has to be careful that the staff counsellor is not expected to do this over and above everything else. That would hardly send out the right kind of message!

A facility needs to be provided where the counsellor can work with the victim. Issues of confidentiality are important here, so discretion is a must. Some organizations actually find it easier to hire a small meeting room if available locally, rather than run the risk of others in the organization knowing what's going on. Ideally the room should be conducive to creating a relaxed atmosphere. Comfortable chairs placed at an angle of 90 degrees to each other encourage people to talk more easily. A small coffee table with refreshments available is also useful. Try to avoid hard chairs facing each other and a desk in between, as this creates a barrier and does not develop equality in the counselling relationship. Try also to ensure that there are no interruptions, and that sufficient time has been allocated for the meeting so that it can be unhurried and relaxed.

When someone has been bullied, the knock-on effect can be enormous. It is highly likely that the individual's close family will be suffering, particularly in serious cases, or where the bullying has been going on for a long time. The health of the victim will have suffered and there will have been behavioural changes. Sometimes it is difficult for those close to the individual to understand what is going on, and relationships could well be under strain. Organizations might want to consider extending their counselling services to immediate family and relatives. This holistic method has much to recommend it, but of course there are implications for financing it.

ROLE OF THE MANAGER

Organizations have a 'duty of care' to their employees, to make sure that their physical, mental and emotional needs are taken care of within the work environment. Managers, therefore, have a responsibility to ensure that the anti-bullying policy is implemented fully.

A manager needs to ensure that staff know how seriously the organization takes the issues of bullying and harassment. This can be achieved by maintaining awareness through brief discussions during team meetings, and by introducing the topic during induction and training sessions.

It is dangerous to assume that no complaints mean there are no problems. Managers need to be vigilant, as the only evidence that something untoward is happening may be subtle behavioural changes. These might be evidenced, for example, when a member of staff becomes rather withdrawn and uncommunicative, easily upset, or they refuse to work with another member of staff. It is part of the manager's role to know and understand their staff. If a manager suspects that there is a problem, they should approach the member of staff in a sensitive manner. People will not necessarily make the first move and report their worries and concerns, but if the manager is seen as being approachable and caring, they may well take advantage of the opportunity to talk about it.

It is useful to remember that someone who is or has been bullied may well feel embarrassed by what has been happening, or even guilty. They may be reluctant to talk about what form the bullying has taken and may even be worried that they are not going to be believed. Managers must be receptive and empathic to their staff, and be prepared to take their concerns seriously.

SURVEYS AND QUESTIONNAIRES

Not all staff will be happy about admitting that they are the victim of bullying, for a variety of reasons. They may be worried that something detrimental will be placed on their personnel file or that they will be perceived as a trouble maker. When people are reluctant to discuss their problems a false picture can be given, and the organization can be misguided into thinking that nothing is wrong.

This is where the use of surveys and questionnaires can prove extremely valuable. If anonymity is maintained then staff may feel more confident to 'tell it how it really is'. The two questionnaires in the toolkit which look at individual bullying behaviour and organizational bullying may be useful (see Tools 8 and 9). There is also a brief survey which can be circulated readily to staff (see Tool 10). This can be useful to disseminate prior to the implementation of an anti-bullying policy, and then perhaps 12 months down the line. Comparisons can then be drawn. Because this survey requires the respondent to answer 'yes' or 'no', a straightforward statistical analysis can be made. This will then provide quantitative as well as qualitative information.

Staff survey

An introduction to a staff survey may go along these lines:

> 'As an organization we are committed to providing an environment where all members of staff are treated with respect and dignity. Our anti-bullying and harassment policy has been developed to make sure that this happens. We need your support in this matter. We are aware that in many instances managers and supervisors may not be aware of any problems, and that staff may be reluctant to talk about what they experience or see. This survey has been designed to gauge the extent to which bullying may or may not be a problem. We would like you to be honest in your responses, and to this end there will be no identifiers which can trace the origin of the script.'

Managers can use the staff survey in the toolkit (see Tool 10), and distribute it among their employees.

It is interesting to get the views and opinions of staff at all levels of the organization. It might be helpful to include some kind of indicator of whether the respondent is in a junior or senior role. However, this would only be possible in a large organization where it would be impossible to work out who had completed the survey. In a smaller company it would be too risky and could compromise anonymity.

SUMMARY

Putting in place an anti-bullying policy, and ensuring that the staff and resources are available to ensure that it runs smoothly, is the 'top down' part of the process. In other words, this is the strategic element which has to be the first step. In order to get the 'bottom up' process working, individuals within the organization need to be confident that they can deal with the problem.

Chapter 4
Guidance for managers and HR professionals

Quite often managers 'feel' that things are not right in an organization, but can not necessarily put their finger on what is wrong. There may be specific unpleasant incidents, such as members of staff being difficult or clashing with others – these are obvious and tangible signs. However, a lot of the time there are no blatant incidents, it is more a malaise or pervading sickness that characterizes an unhealthy organization. Identifying where it comes from or who is responsible is almost like trying to knit fog.

When this is the case, people find it very difficult to tackle the situation. They may well have problems in convincing senior management that there is indeed a problem because the evidence is thin or woolly, or examples of bad behaviour seem trivial and inconsequential.

The first thing to do is to trust your instinct. If you feel that things are not right then your judgement is probably correct. Gut instinct isn't something that is plucked out of thin air, it is an accumulation of past experiences and observations. In other words, you might not as yet be able to identify what is wrong, but you *know* something is.

The second course of action is to examine the situation in a more objective and analytical way. This is the search for evidence to support your hunch.

Managers have a responsibility to tackle bullying on two fronts. They must feel confident that they can deal with someone who makes a complaint about bullying in a professional, sensitive and objective manner; and they must be vigilant when it comes to identifying bullying behaviours and be able to know what to do if they occur. In other words, managers need to take both a reactive and preventative approach.

Earlier chapters have hopefully given some insight into why bullying occurs, but we need to look more specifically at what behaviours or traits managers need to look out for.

WHAT TO LOOK FOR IN A DEPARTMENT/SECTION

In a department/section, the signs that bullying may be occurring are:

- Low morale, lack of team spirit.
- A general air of unpleasantness – these symptoms may develop if the department has recently had a change of leadership.
- Irritability, touchiness and lack of patience especially over minor issues – again, is this recent or long standing?
- Mistrust and suspicion between colleagues – this is especially significant if they used to be willing and helpful.
- Selfishness – people trying to protect themselves.
- Staff leaving or requesting transfers or sideways moves. Reasons given may seem plausible, as people are unwilling to admit that they are being bullied.
- People moving to a job which is below their capabilities – they may be looking for breathing space or have had their confidence undermined.
- Are people always watching their backs? Does hypersensitivity or hypervigilance pervade?

HOW TO SPOT A VICTIM OF BULLYING

The following are signs of a victim of bullying:

- Loss of self-confidence in someone who has always come across as capable and responsible.
- Physiological and psychological symptoms (often identified as stress related), including tearfulness, anxiety, depression, lack of motivation, illness and inability to sleep or eat properly. If an individual has not exhibited these symptoms before, then there is a problem.
- Family problems – especially with a partner, but could also be with children, stemming from changes in behaviour patterns and inability to cope.
- Behaviour which is out of character – this is easier when you have known a person well or for a long time.
- Phrases such as 'What's the point?', 'I don't care', 'Things will never change', 'You can't win'.
- Increasing use of abusive language stemming from anger, frustration and resentment of the situation.
- Unexplained absences from work and while at work.
- Mistakes, errors and poor performance in someone who is usually reliable.
- Apathy and dejection.

HOW TO SPOT A BULLY

The following are signs of a bully at work:

- Pointing out other people's mistakes, quite often in public, while minimizing their own.
- Shouting, swearing at, abusing staff for trivialities in front of colleagues – or in private.
- Disregarding people's rights, for example denying leave entitlement on flimsy grounds (or none at all), pressuring people to work long hours or

return to work prematurely when off sick, setting unrealistic objectives and targets, changing the goalposts.
- Looking out for themselves at the expense of others.
- Scapegoating individuals – constant blame, fault finding and nit-picking.
- Sending people to Coventry, ignoring them or 'tutting' when they enter the room.
- Selective memory – only recalling information and facts that are useful to themselves or show them in a good light.
- Untrustworthiness – making promises that aren't kept, saying one thing and doing something else, setting others up to fail.
- Poor judgement – being unable to take a balanced view on issues.
- Poor listening skills, usually thinking through what they want to say to cover their tracks – disregarding the thoughts and feelings of others.
- Difficulty in acknowledging and valuing positive traits in others – jealousy of their achievements or circumstances.
- Finding it hard to say 'thank you' and exchange pleasantries with people (unless used as a manipulative tool).
- Taking credit for the work of others – inflating their achievements to bolster their ego while putting others down.
- A poor delegator, but will have no compunction about dumping work on others – often with unrealistic expectations and time frames.
- Will find it hard to take criticism, even if it's constructive and will see it as a personal sleight or affront. Can be full of their own self-importance.
- Will find it hard to admit when they're in the wrong and will not back down or retract what they have said or done.
- Usually a poor communicator with limited social skills. However, some bullies can be very smooth and plausible and extremely skilled at twisting things round to their advantage.

This is not an exhaustive list, but gives an indication of what to look out for and to identify specifics rather than generalities.

WHAT STEPS TO TAKE TO SORT THINGS OUT

A good starting point is to introduce an anti-bullying policy (as discussed earlier), making sure that there is commitment from senior management. Following the procedures and guidelines in Chapters 2 and 3 should help you to do this. Similarly, the surveys and questionnaires in the toolkit will give you the baseline data you need to strengthen the case for taking this action. If tackled carefully and thoroughly, the message given will be that the company/organization values its employees.

In addition to an anti-bullying policy there are three key areas which need addressing: training, support systems and appraisals. These require a top down/bottom up approach in that they need to be tackled at an organizational, group and individual level.

Training and support systems

Staff should be aware of what the organization is doing to combat bullying. This can be done through a programme of awareness raising seminars and workshops. However, training should not just focus on the issues of bullying *per se*, it should be much broader and more comprehensive. Bullies often lack people management skills and have not been trained in how to get the best from people. Their own interpersonal and communication skills are often weak, and they rely on methods which get results in the short term rather than learning more effective strategies which take into consideration the long-term view as well.

In a similar vein those who are victims of bullying often do not have the skills to deal with it. They may behave passively rather than assertively, or find it difficult to regain their confidence and self-esteem. They may have a misguided view of what good management is and could be inadvertently perpetuating the problem.

When people are aware of alternative ways of doing things, they are less likely to rely on what they perceive as 'effective strategies'.

In some ways the term 'training' is inadequate and misleading as it implies a narrow interpretation of what is actually 'learning'. When applied to technical skills it is useful, but when looking at ways to change behaviour, training needs to approach the issue from a wider perspective.

There are a number of approaches to learning and people development which do not solely rely on 'classroom' activities. In fact the traditional model of an intensive two- or three-day course has been proven to be only marginally effective, as what is learned in the training room does not necessarily transfer to the workplace.

An holistic model is needed, that is, a programme which evolves over time and which uses a series or combination of learning and support methods. Managers should consider using some or indeed all of the following.

Experiential workshops

In-house workshops promote group identity and cohesion and can offer a safe environment in which to tackle difficult and complex issues. A word of warning, however! A skilled facilitator will be needed who is familiar with group dynamics and can manage diversity and potential conflict.

The content of such workshops may vary but should contain a strong element of the importance of good interpersonal skills and communication. In some organizations these are seen as 'soft skills' and by inference are perceived as being less important than, for example, product knowledge. However, if an organization has problems with bullying or is supporting (albeit unwittingly) a negative culture, it is imperative that these subjects are tackled.

One-to-one coaching

Coaching *per se* is not necessarily a means to help an individual tackle bullying. However, if an individual has, for example, poor time management, is disorganized or has problems being assertive with colleagues, coaching on a one-to-one basis is a useful way to improve work competencies and reduce pressure.

This is usually undertaken by the line manager or sometimes an HR professional. Good coaching sessions focus on individual needs by establishing a personal development plan which addresses two or three development goals.

It is an enabling process in that it empowers the individual to take control of the situation.

One-to-one mentoring

In a sense this is similar to coaching, but is seen as a process which supports learning and development in the individual's long-term career and possibly external influences. It is an empathic and supportive relationship and is usually taken on by a senior member of staff who is not the individual's line manager. In a mentoring situation it may transpire that someone is not suited to a particular environment, for example high pressured sales. A mentor can then help the individual to look at possible alternatives. Someone who is being bullied in one situation might find that they would cope better in a different work environment entirely.

Psychometric tests

Psychometric tests analyse behaviour, personality and work styles. They are helpful in identifying strengths and weaknesses and can be used as a starting point for individual or group work.

One-to-one counselling

This can focus on different levels, from providing a listening ear or a sounding-board, to tackling difficult and complex attitudes and behaviours. As part of the learning process it can be a very valuable tool. Some organizations offer employee assistance programmes (EAPs) which either give support over the telephone or face to face. If counsellors are used to support victims of bullying, or individuals who bully, they must be qualified and experienced. If staff within an organization take on a counselling role they must be aware of their own limitations and be prepared to refer to a specialist if necessary.

Work shadowing

Working alongside others can give individuals valuable insight into what their job entails. Quite often managers become too far removed from the nitty gritty of what happens on a daily basis and are out of touch. Stepping into the shoes of a junior member of staff can help alleviate pressure bullying as the realization dawns that expectations are unrealistic.

Buddy system

A 'buddy' system can be very useful for new staff or for someone who moves to a different department or takes on a new role. Similarly, having someone as a point of reference can prevent problems such as bullying happening in the first place. The 'buddy' is not necessarily a manager or supervisor (in fact in some ways it is better if they are not). Their job is more of a befriender and helper. This system can help the new person to settle in more quickly and give them someone to turn to if there are problems. Buddies need to be selected carefully in that they should be staff who have energy and enthusiasm. There is little value in using someone who is cynical and demotivated. The amount of time that the two spend together will vary from organization to organization, but it is helpful to set aside a specific time on a regular basis. Initially this could be weekly, or even daily, but will pan out to less intensive contact after a few weeks. It can be done informally over a coffee or lunch break which reinforces the parity of the relationship rather than the notion of expert and novice.

Focus groups

These can be convened for a number of purposes, for example examining specific work processes or looking into the feasibility of introducing new techniques or expanding the business. In the context of bullying, focus groups can look at attitudes in the organization or analyse the culture of a company or even a department. They can report findings to senior managers and/or put together recommendations. The purpose of the group will dictate its composition. In the context of using a focus group to help promote a positive culture within an organization, it is useful to bear a few things in mind:

1. Have a clear set of goals. People need to understand what they are doing, why and by when.
2. Consider using a cross-section of levels within the organization, for example vertical grouping, or select staff from different departments.
3. Research indicates that group identity is enhanced when members have a purpose and meet frequently.
4. What will be the outcome? Will this be a consultative group which puts forward a series of recommendations, or will there be some decision-making element?
5. Will there be a designated leader or a division of responsibilities with a facilitator?
6. If using a focus group, spend some time researching the literature on group dynamics and processes. This will ensure that things run smoothly and potential pitfalls are recognized early on.

Using a focus group within an organization can be a very powerful tool. It involves and empowers staff from different levels and departments, and can help to break down any 'them and us' divisions.

The brief of the group should not only be clear, but be worthwhile. In other words whatever issue the group is looking into should have value and relevance, otherwise it will be perceived as shallow and superficial. This will do more harm than good. It should be taken seriously by the ultimate decision-makers in the organization, in the sense that something should happen as a result of the work that has been done. Expectations will be raised, and if nothing comes of it morale and enthusiasm will flag.

Appraisals

Many organizations have appraisal systems, but not all are useful and productive. Many companies and institutions regard their appraisal systems as being a nuisance, a waste of time and quite often counter productive. It is often a stick that is used to drive its employees, and although it purports to be a two-way process between appraiser and appraisee, this is not always the case.

Perhaps the first point that needs consideration is that an appraisal system which is only used annually usually has little impact. Comments that were made twelve months previously, or goals or targets that are set without any monitoring or evaluation, become meaningless. Unfortunately many of us have been through this process and it colours our judgement. If an informal appraisal interview takes place annually then it must be followed up with regular meetings between the manager and the employee. This should be done at least monthly when the situation can be reviewed, amendments made and new targets set. Regular contact can enhance the relationship between the manager and his or her staff.

If a manager has a large number of employees directly under him or her, then this ongoing process could be delegated to supervisors or team leaders. They can then report back perhaps on a quarterly basis. If the manager feels that the employee is reasonably competent in a number of areas, and yet reports from the supervisor suggest otherwise, there could be cause for investigating matters further.

With any appraisal process there must be uniformity and consistency. This means that anyone taking on the role of appraiser should receive training in the appropriate skills. In one organization I know of, one of the managers never rated anyone above a 'B' grade (out of A to D). This was because he felt that not only could no one be perfect, but if the employee was in a junior grade it meant that they still had some way to go in terms of experience and advancement. In effect he was not rating the job itself, but placing the employee on a level according to the rank of the job. His colleagues worked differently, giving top grades if they felt the individual deserved it – within the job that they were being appraised for. Not surprisingly this created all sorts of problems within the organization, particularly as the manager concerned was the head of one of the larger departments.

Another important issue worth raising is the fact that most appraisal systems are manager/subordinate based. They rely on a more senior and/or experienced member of staff making a judgement about a junior member of staff. In some instances the junior can agree or disagree with the assessment, and grades or ratings may be changed accordingly, but there still remains this imbalance in terms of power. Over the last five to ten years there have been moves to introduce a more comprehensive system of appraisal. This is widely referred to and usually known as 'multi-rater' or '360 degree' appraisal.

In essence, what this means is that an individual is assessed or rated not only by their boss, but by their peers and juniors. There is also an element of ipsative (or self-) assessment. Anyone interested in implementing such a system would be well advised to look carefully at how it can be done. As with most things there are pros and cons (see Table 4.1).

The benefits of a 360 degree appraisal system probably outweigh the difficulties, especially when trying to eradicate bullying from an organization. It can help to overcome the thorny problem of how to tackle senior personnel who are bullies, but who have in a sense been allowed to carry on because there is no effective system of accountability.

If a bully is identified through this process, it will not be an easy task to get them to admit that their behaviour leaves a lot to be desired. There may well be surprise (whether genuine or feigned), denial and anger. Whoever takes on the role of working with such an individual, needs to be prepared for this.

Some useful pointers

The following may be useful in dealing with someone who uses bullying tactics. The information gleaned from the appraisal ratings of others should be taken as the basis for the discussion.

Table 4.1 Pros and cons of 360 degree appraisals

Pros	Cons
• Gives a much more comprehensive picture of an individual in a number of roles (boss, colleague, subordinate). • Identifies, for example, whether a manager is skilled at managing his staff or just gives that impression to his boss. • Applies to all staff. The MD or directors are not exempt, and their leadership/management styles are examined. • Identifies team players (or not as the case may be). • Can form the basis of more specific and targeted training and development. • Ratings are done anonymously (from junior ranks especially), so that people can speak freely. • More objective analysis than usual appraisal system – especially if external consultants are involved.	• Can be very threatening to individuals, particularly senior levels who may not have been appraised for some time. • Needs to be thought through very carefully and as a development of the existing system. From no appraisals to 360 degree may be too much of a quantum leap. • External consultants may have to be employed to facilitate the process initially. • Can pinpoint specific behaviours which will need to be modified or developed, and therefore is not for those who do not intend to do anything. • More time-consuming than usual system, a lot of information is generated, which might prove to be unwieldy. • Will raise expectations that something good will come from it – not to be considered unless total commitment is there. • Who will give feedback to the MD? Again, possibly need to consider external professionals as it may not be politic to use HR department or personnel.

It is always easier to use data gathered from an assessment to get your point across, rather than making a comment yourself (the same applies when giving feedback from psychometric tests). In other words, it is better to say:

> 'The results of this appraisal seem to suggest that you have some difficulties with (delegating, setting realistic goals, communicating with others) etc.'

than

> 'You have a problem with ...'

Depersonalizing the feedback is easier for the person giving it, and less threatening for the individual receiving it. As a rule of thumb in any feedback situation, the following format should be used:

Positive – Negative – Positive

Positive – comment on the good things that have come out of the appraisal. Praise any areas that deserve positive comments – even bullies have their good points! It may be that the individual works very hard (albeit possibly not constructively) and puts in some long hours. Acknowledge the commitment.

Negative – here is the meat of the problem. Again, the results of the appraisal should be used to focus on areas of concern. 'The results of this appraisal seem to indicate ...' There may be many areas that the individual needs to work on, but you should try and focus on two or three general issues at this stage, for example communication, interpersonal skills, personal organization. It is not helpful to reel off a whole list of misdemeanours as you are likely to be met with resistance and non-compliance. You may well find this anyway, but you need to try and minimize the possibility. The purpose of this feedback is to move forward, not 'beat someone up'.

Take one of the points and identify a couple of behaviours that you can get the individual to look at, for example:

Communication

1 You seem to find it hard to tell people when they have done well at something.
2 You seem to be perceived as being rather distant and not easy to approach.

Please note that the original comments behind these two points may have been something like this:

- She always finds fault with our work, nothing we do is ever right.
- She's stuck up. She's not interested in us or what we have to cope with, all she wants is the job doing.

By phrasing your comments in a less emotive way you are more likely to gain acceptance from the individual you are dealing with. If they refuse to accept this analysis they may say something defensive like:

'I don't agree with that at all, it's a load of rubbish. Of course I praise my staff.'

or

'Who said that about me? They don't know what they're talking about.'

Keep calm! Make sure that your response is given in such a way that you are not going to get into an argument or heated discussion. The conversation might go something like this:

Interviewer:

'That's interesting, it sounds as if you don't agree with this analysis.'

Individual:

'No I don't, it's not true. All that stuff is distorted. It's only someone else's view, it's not what really happens.'

Interviewer:

'Okay, I take your point that this information is based on the perception of others. Can you give me some examples of when and how you comment on the work of your staff?'

Individual:

'Well, only the other day I told Sarah I was pleased with her work.'

Interviewer:

'That's good. What had she done, and why were you so pleased?'

Individual:

'Oh I can't remember now. It was something to do with getting something done on time – I don't know. That was last week, you know how busy we are, I can't think that far back.'

At this point the interviewer will have a good idea that either the individual is making it up or it did happen, but many moons ago! Asking for clarification or evidence to support their objections usually tells you whether it is real or whether they are trying to bluff their way out of a situation.

Let's continue the conversation ...

Interviewer:

> 'Right, it looks as though you do try and comment on the good work your staff do. How do you think you can develop that some more? What can you do to ensure that it happens on a regular basis?'

Now you can negotiate some targets. You might want to introduce the idea of playing up the positive and minimizing the negative since people respond better to positive suggestions. Agree a time frame when you will meet again, making sure the individual is very clear about what you are asking them to do. Write it down and get a copy to them as quickly as possible. Sometimes with resistant behaviours it is helpful to make it into a 'mini' contract, which both parties sign. This is especially useful if the manager is going to do something to help the individual meet their targets.

Remember the acronym SMART (see Figure 4.1).

Figure 4.1 SMART objectives

S   –   Specific

M   –   Measurable

A   –   Agreed

R   –   Realistic

T   –   Time agreed

Use these criteria when setting goals.

Finally ...

Positive – finish the session on a positive note. There may be something else that you can comment on work wise, or you may want to introduce something unconnected with work. For example, asking about their recent holiday, their children or even if they've seen the latest James Bond film or have been to a new restaurant. All this helps to complete the interview on good terms and a positive note.

WORKING WITH A BULLY

If as a manager you are going to work directly with an individual who has been identified as a bully, you need to gauge their ability to engage in any kind of plan of action you may have in mind. There is little point in using any of the material suggested in the toolkit if they are not motivated to change. Unless they are ready to change they will go through the motions, but won't necessarily believe that they have a problem.

There are four levels of readiness that people go through during a successful behaviour change:

1 **Oblivious** – It is not that people are unwilling to look for solutions, they just don't see that there's a problem in the first place. They deny there is any need to change and resist any attempts to help them.

2 **Contemplation** – People at this stage begin to see that they need to change and have begun to think about how they might go about it. They will think about it and talk about it, but the motivation to actually do anything is half-hearted.

3 **Preparation** – In this stage people start to focus on finding new and better ways to improve on a situation and are eager to generate solutions. Interestingly some individuals will be pushed into this state of readiness by a dramatic event. This might be a crisis in their personal lives, a disaster at work or the threat of losing their job. This is the time for putting together a specific and detailed plan of action.

4 **Action** – This is when visible change begins to take place. Individuals will have 'bought into' the plan and will start to change their thought patterns and behaviour.

It is worth pointing out that when working with a bully it might need something as dramatic as the real possibility that the individual could be sidelined into another department, lose their status, be offered a job with less responsibility and power or even face the threat of being dismissed, unless they change. This might sound harsh, but in essence the individual concerned is being given the opportunity to take responsibility for their actions – or face the consequences. They do have a choice.

However, if it becomes apparent that this is the only avenue open to you as a manager, the whole situation must be handled with tact and sensitivity. If threats are made, for example 'If you don't change you're going to lose your job', then your behaviour becomes no better than that of the bully.

HELPING THE VICTIMS OF BULLYING

The appraisal system can identify the victims of bullying in much the same way as it highlights the existence of bullies. However, victims of bullying can be identified in other ways such as by the individual approaching a manager directly (always assuming that their manager is not the source of the problem), through a third party (for example, a colleague or supervisor) or by confiding in someone they trust.

Assuming that as a manager you are part of the solution and not the problem, there are a number of things you can do to help the victims of bullying:

1 Please take what the individual says seriously. Bullying is emotional and sometimes physical abuse. It thrives in environments where people choose to ignore what is going on, or avoid getting involved. It relies on the victim keeping quiet (much the same as sexual abuse continues because of fear and shame), and not confronting what is going on. Remember also that bullying cuts across all levels within an organization. It can emanate from the managing director or even the office junior. Although it is more likely to be

an individual in a position of power, this is not necessarily the case. Bullies acquire a following (be a bully or be bullied), but sometimes those in more lowly positions can make someone's life a misery. Keep an open mind and don't prejudge, you may not have seen any evidence to support the allegation, but this does not mean it hasn't happened. Make sure that it is investigated thoroughly and fairly so that those who speak out feel that the problem is being addressed.

2 Make sure you allocate sufficient time in a private place with no interruptions for your meeting with the individual. If you cannot see them immediately agree a mutually convenient time to meet as soon as possible.

3 An initial interview should not focus on an assessment or analysis of the problem. It is about listening and encouraging the individual to talk and open up.

4 Use counselling techniques in this and subsequent meetings. This means active listening, that is, checking and showing you have understood by paraphrasing, reflecting back and asking for clarification. Make sure you do not 'manage' the situation, by taking control through giving solutions.

5 Familiarize yourself with the material in this book that focuses on assessment and analysis. Look at models of behaviour, in particular the transactional analysis model and the PUCA model in Chapter 6. The tools for analysing behaviour, for example the questionnaires and surveys, will also help. These will give you the necessary grounding in understanding why people react as they do to events and situations. It will also help if you are dealing with a bully. Photocopy appropriate material for the individual concerned. Discuss the information with them; ask for their views and opinions. Help individuals to understand that there is nothing 'wrong' with them and it is not their fault. Be careful not to perpetuate the victim mode, you need to be encouraging them to take control of the situation, but with your support. Think of an analogy of scaffolding. It is built around the individual to give them support, you help them to gain strength and confidence and when they can stand alone, the scaffolding is dismantled. You must guard against creating dependency. Your job is to empower, not to take over – however tempting this might be.

6 It is more difficult to view bullies as possible victims, especially when their behaviour has caused so much pain and destruction. However, not all bullies are sociopaths with personality disorders. Some will respond to intervention, and will be able to assimilate new behaviours.

7 Use the questionnaire in the toolkit which identifies a person's preferred mode of response to threatening and challenging behaviour (see Tool 6). Ask the individual to complete it as honestly as they can, and use the information gained to identify which tools would be appropriate, for example improving confidence, assertiveness or relaxation techniques.

8 Work with the individual on a one-to-one basis, going through the material selected from the toolkit to ensure that they understand and feel comfortable with it. Reassure and support them. Never ask anyone to do something they are reluctant to do, look for alternatives and help them to build up their confidence bit by bit.

9 Meet with them on a regular basis. Initially this may be weekly, but as they become more confident and start to take control of their situation, it could be fortnightly or monthly.

10 Use the SMART technique (see Figure 4.1, page 52) to ensure that they achieve success. When in doubt, start with things that the individual feels can be more readily achieved, even if these are small steps. Once things start to improve, success will breed success.

Psychological debriefing

This is a technique which is used by psychologists and experienced counsellors and has its roots in clinical psychology. When someone has gone through a traumatic experience (trauma being defined here as out of the ordinary and unexpected), a trained psychologist would go through the incident with those involved as quickly as possible after it occurred. This is usually within 48 hours. Large-scale tragedies immediately spring to mind, such as Lockerbie, the King's Cross fire or Hillsborough, but it is a technique that can be used in less dramatic, but no less important or difficult situations.

If a member of staff is physically assaulted at work or is psychologically intimidated and as a consequence they are shocked, upset and hurt it may be useful to consider debriefing. This can be done in a reasonably straightforward way if the incident involves external clients, but it is a bit trickier if it is an internal problem. You may want to consider an external service provider and using off-site premises to ensure confidentiality and discretion. However, it must be emphasized that psychological debriefing is a very specialized technique and needs to be done by someone who is qualified and experienced. Support may be available through an employee assistance programme (EAP), the health service or private practitioners.

SUMMARY

There are a number of things that managers can do both in a preventative way and in response to a disclosure of bullying.

Although it is possible for a victim of bullying to tackle this on their own, it can be very difficult to do so. The next chapter looks at how this can be done, but even if the victim does confront the bully and wants to sort it out themselves, it can be a nerve-racking experience. If you are a manager and suspect that someone is being bullied or is bullying, it might not be appropriate for you to intervene straight away. Your attentions may not be welcome and you could make the situation worse. It is better to draw people's attention to the fact that there is a resource available to them. A copy of this manual should be available for people to access freely – this may be in a library or resource centre, or in the staff room or rest room. Staff can be reminded of its existence during team meetings and so on, alongside any other material you want them to know about.

At a corporate level you will find more resources for dealing with bullying in your organization in the toolkit. The matrix at the beginning of the toolkit section (see pages 70–72) will help you to work out exactly which tools will be the most appropriate to use, and in what circumstances.

Chapter 5
Guidance for individuals

This chapter is intended to help those who are on the receiving end of bullying and also, to a degree, those who may be using bullying tactics.

EXAMINING YOUR SITUATION

Are you happy and fulfilled at work? Do you enjoy your job and have good relationships with your colleagues and manager? If you answer 'yes' to these questions then you probably don't need to read any further.

However, if you are:

- unhappy
- unfulfilled
- hate your job
- experiencing difficult relationships

... you might want to think about these questions:

1. Do you think you are being bullied?
2. Are you using bullying tactics or techniques?

The two are not mutually exclusive. If you are already in a position of responsibility you might be experiencing unacceptable behaviour from your immediate boss which is then cascading down to your staff. If this is the case you will benefit from reading the rest of this chapter and accessing the appropriate strategies in the toolkit.

Consider the following behaviours:

1. Having your options and views ignored.
2. Withholding information affecting performance.
3. Exposed to an unmanageable workload.
4. Given tasks with unreasonable deadlines.
5. Ordered to do work below your competence.
6. Attempts to find fault with your work.
7. Humiliated or ridiculed in connection with work.
8. Being ignored or facing a hostile reaction when you approach.
9. Excessive monitoring of your work.
10. Spreading of gossip or rumours about you.

You may not have thought that these are bullying behaviours, but the study by the University of Manchester Institute of Science and Technology (UMIST), whose findings were published in March 2000 (see Further reading and useful contacts, page 183), list these behaviours above as the ones most commonly reported by people who had suffered bullying. If you are experiencing any of these behaviours, or indeed if you are guilty of treating your staff in this way, then you will benefit from reading the rest of this chapter and accessing the appropriate strategies and techniques in the toolkit.

However, for the most part, this chapter is geared towards those individuals who are being bullied either because they are good at their jobs and popular, and the bully resents and envies this; or because they are being targeted by a bully who is predisposed through temperament, personality or life experiences to take out their frustrations and inadequacies on others. Some people may not be particularly familiar with self-help material. Not everyone feels comfortable with trying out new ways of doing things, or analysing what is going on. If this is the case, then a trusted friend or colleague could be brought in to collaborate in trying out the strategies in the toolkit.

When you feel ready to do something about the situation, read on! You will gain insight and confidence which will enable you to deal with the problem.

CONFRONTING THE PROBLEM

In essence there are two ways of dealing with the problem of being bullied – either confront the bully directly or seek help from someone. Doing nothing about it and putting up with the situation is a third option, but not one to be recommended. Looking for another job, resigning and taking early retirement are further options. However, although they get rid of the problem of bullying, they can create other difficulties. These can include sustained and prolonged feelings of inadequacy, lack of self-worth, bitterness and hardship (both emotional and financial). If you can summon up the courage to face the problem, you are less likely to experience these effects – even if ultimately you decide to get another job, work part-time or whatever. It will then be your choice and not something which you have been forced into.

Dealing with it yourself

If you do decide to do something about it, you may want to deal with it yourself, for a number of reasons. You may feel embarrassed by the fact that you are being bullied or ashamed to talk to anyone about it. Perhaps the bully is a female manager and you are a male employee. Do you feel that you are a wimp or that it is a sign of weakness if you involve others? Think carefully about why you want to do this completely by yourself. Make a list of the pros and cons and try and be honest about your motives.

This is not to say that it is wrong or inadvisable to go it alone, but it is difficult. You might want to consider confiding in your partner or a trusted friend. They can at least give you moral support even if they are not actively involved in the process.

You might want to consider taking a colleague along with you when you tackle the individual concerned. You can explain that they are there as an observer to what is being said. It is perhaps more prudent to ask someone who is not a close friend to do this – perhaps a union representative or someone you do not work directly with. If your supporter is seen as being partisan, then their version of events could be interpreted as being biased. This might make things more difficult for you.

Whichever way you want to do it, it is important to think things through beforehand. Decide what you need from this individual and how you are going to put it across. Use the techniques of Broken Record and Scripting that are described in the toolkit (see Tools 11 and 13) to help you do this.

Approach the individual concerned and ask them if you can have a few minutes of their time to speak to them about a private matter. Select the timing of this very carefully as you are more likely to make headway if they are not harassed or dealing with something which is urgent, for example. If they cannot accommodate you there and then, set a time which is mutually convenient. Don't be drawn into discussing what it is about, just reiterate that you need to speak with them. If they respond aggressively, for example 'I haven't got the time, I'm rushed off my feet', keep calm and maintain a level tone of voice. Acknowledge that you appreciate that they are busy, but that it won't take long. You will need to be firm and quietly insistent. If necessary, say that you would be prepared to speak with them after work. Emphasize that this is important and that you would appreciate their time.

This approach may be disconcerting to the bully. They may be curious as to what you want or suspicious that you are up to something. You may find that they set a time only to cancel it at the last minute. Be patient. This is usually evidence of gamesmanship. In other words:

> 'I'm in control and *you're* not going to dictate terms to *me*.'

You will need to persevere. Set another time, and another if you have to. Don't rise to the bait and keep your cool. You may find that eventually you are given five minutes (begrudgingly), but it is enough to state your case.

When you have your 'five minutes' you need to make the most of it. Remember:

- **Body language** – don't slouch if you are standing up. Plant feet firmly a little way apart, put your shoulders back and give direct eye contact. If you are invited to sit down, don't fold your arms defensively or curl up into a foetal position.
- **Voice** – maintain a level tone, neither whispering nor shouting. Practise beforehand what you are going to say so that you are well rehearsed and it comes out fluently.

If you act in a confident manner you will feel more confident, and more importantly you will be perceived by the other person as being confident. Think of the swan gliding across the surface of a lake. Its feet can be paddling frantically below the surface, but all you see is the serene image of a bird that is totally in control! Try this out for yourself, it does work.

There may be a number of ways in which you are being bullied. These might include:

- constantly criticized for petty or trivial things
- demeaned and put down in front of colleagues
- shouted at
- singled out to do boring, routine jobs that should be shared out amongst everyone

… and so on.

State that you are unhappy with the way you are being treated and how this makes you feel. Then back it up with a couple of specific examples. State then that you want (not that you would like) this behaviour to stop. Your statement might go something like this:

> 'I am very unhappy about the way that you are treating me. I find your intimidating behaviour distressing and totally unacceptable. You put me down in front of others, for example yesterday you said I must have only half a brain cell to imagine that my quarterly report was even adequate. I want you to stop behaving towards me in this way at once.'

It is unlikely that the bully will accept what you say graciously and admit their behaviour, so you must be prepared for a variety of actions and responses. Some of these may happen at the time of the interview, others may come later. Be prepared for some, if not all of the following processes.

Surprise

This could be the first time that they have been challenged. The surprise may be genuine if, for example, they are a pressure bully, and you may find that they are taken aback and have not realized the impact their behaviour has had on you.

However, it is more likely to be an instinctive response. Look out for the following phrases:

> 'Who, me?'

> 'You must be mistaken.'

> 'Are you sure you haven't misinterpreted things?'

> 'Are you absolutely sure you've got the right end of the stick?'

Denial

This is a common response and stems from our primitive instinct for self-preservation. To deny that we have done anything is to abdicate responsibility for our actions.

Projection

This is where the bully projects their own behaviour onto the other person to deflect responsibility. Stand firm, these are bullying tactics. Projection statements may sound something like:

> 'You really do have an attitude, don't you?'

> 'You're the one with the problem, not me.'

> 'You've always been a trouble maker.'

Alarm

The bully may sense that they could be cornered and may look for ways of 'escaping'. They may come up with phrases which sound as though they are prepared to look for solutions:

> 'I'm sure we can work this out.'

> 'There is no need to upset yourself.'
> (*even though your demeanour suggests otherwise*)

> 'We don't need to involve anyone else in this, do we?'

At this point you need to consider whether the individual is trustworthy and you can work things out between you, or whether it is yet another tactic to get them off the hook, by playing on your sympathy.

Your response might be:

> 'I am happy to work things out, but I would like to ask Mr A to be present at our next meeting to act as an independent observer.'

or:

> 'I'm glad that you want to get this sorted. You wouldn't have any objections then to putting in writing what we agree will happen?'

Watch out for their reaction. If they are sincere they will accept either of these reasonable requests. If they object, be careful. If they want you to agree to a course of action that is neither witnessed or documented and signed, it is all too easy for them to renege on their promises and then deny all knowledge of the agreement. Furthermore, it could give more reason and opportunity for them to scheme and plot against you.

If you stand your ground you might find that the bully uses additional tactics to undermine you and make you drop the whole thing. These tactics are:

- **Sympathy** – making you feel bad by letting you know how hard things are for them. They may well be going through a tough time, but this doesn't excuse their behaviour.

- **Threat and provocation** – which are usually implied to frighten the accuser, for example 'I will have to report you to the MD.' The inference may be that the bully has the MD's support, but this may not necessarily be the case. Provocation may come in the guise of emotionally driven statements, for example 'Your behaviour is extremely immature, you're embarrassing yourself.' This is also a form of projection and you need to remain in control and stay calm.
(Tim Field – *Bully in Sight*)

Whatever the bully says or threatens you must keep a record of it. Immediately after the interaction write down as much as you can. You will not be able to remember everything verbatim, but some statements may stick in your mind. Alternatively, you may want to make a tape recording of the interview. If this is done without the knowledge of the other party, you could be accused of being devious, unprofessional or worse. However, if the tape recording is done *with* the knowledge of the other party, the bully is hardly likely to say anything detrimental on tape, and it may inflame the situation. In a sense this course of action is down to the individual. If you do decide to go ahead and tape the conversation without the knowledge of the other person, it would be wise to use it only as a last resort and preferably after you have consulted a lawyer.

When it becomes apparent that you as the victim are not going to give up or give in, things may 'hot up'. The bully will use attack as a form of defence, magnifying the so-called misdemeanours of the victim while minimizing their own shortcomings. They will create, or attempt to create, doubt and confusion as to what has really gone on and use diversion tactics to deflect the spotlight from them. Throughout all of this it is important to focus on the facts – what the bully actually did and what they actually said, when this happened, where it happened and who (if anyone) was present. This is your evidence.

Should things go down the route of a grievance and disciplinary procedure or to a tribunal, the bully could well surrender in the hope of winning sympathy, leniency or mitigation, or he or she may feign innocence and play the part of the victim (see Table 5.1).

It takes a lot to see this for what it is – an abdication of responsibility and inability to accept the consequences of their actions. However, these tactics often work because people who do not think and behave as a bully feel guilty. They start to believe that perhaps they are being too hard on the individual – or even begin to question whether they've made a mistake.

Don't be distracted, keep your eye on the ball and stick to the evidence – hard data not emotional manoeuvrings.

Perhaps now it becomes more apparent why it is not easy to deal with a bully on your own without any support. A bully will not be concerned with justice or fair play and you may well find it hard to stand up to the sneaky and underhand tactics they use. Your mind set will be different from theirs, they do not play by the rules.

If confronting a bully face to face fills you with dread, but you still want to try and sort it out without involving someone else in the organization, you could write a letter. The format would be as much the same as presenting your case verbally – this is what is happening, this is how it makes me feel, it is unacceptable and I want it to stop. Don't justify yourself, you do not need to give reasons. Focus on the facts. Complete the letter by stating that if the bullying and/or harassment does not stop you will take further action. Be sure to keep a copy of anything you write. Be prepared for the reactions discussed in this chapter, with the added strong possibility that things will get worse. If this happens you must be prepared to take another course of action.

Table 5.1 Examples of tactics used by a bully

I surrender	I am a victim
• I had no idea. • I'm really, really sorry. • It won't happen again. • It wasn't intentional.	• Why is this happening to me? • What have I done to deserve this?

(Reproduced by kind permission of Tim Field – *Bully in Sight*)

Seeking help

It may be that the situation has deteriorated to the point where you feel you cannot tackle the bully by yourself. If this is the case you need to decide who you are going to speak to and when. It really does help your case if you have some documented evidence to back up what you are going to say. This can be in the form of a diary or journal with the following information:

- dates and times
- who was present and witnesses
- what happened (factual)
- what was said
- what you did or the outcome.

Because bullying is often insidious and cumulative, incidents in isolation seem trivial and inconsequential. However, if a picture is built up over a period of time, these small incidents become a part of the whole and can then be seen in their true light – as systematic and calculated. Take for instance this true case study.

> Mrs X is a highly competent and creative teacher who gets amazing results from her students – whatever the level of their ability. She is conscientious and caring and works hard for them and also her department. Enter a new head of department who is younger and less experienced. She is a good teacher, but does not have the same spark and charisma. Over a period of approximately two years the head of department systematically targets Mrs X with a bullying campaign. Reports are 'lost' and have to be done again, her timetable is disrupted, important messages are not passed on, unrealistic deadlines are set for completion of work and fault is found with lesson plans. Added to which, the other members of the department are sucked into the campaign.
>
> This leads to uncomfortable silences or 'tuts' of disapproval when Mrs X enters the staff room. Verbal communication is terse and she is excluded from discussions and planning sessions. From being a confident and outgoing individual Mrs X is reduced to tears, self-doubt and believes that there is something wrong with her. She lapses into depression and is off work for six months. During this time she is able to reappraise the situation and see it for what it is. She goes back to work and actively looks for another job in a new school, which she gets without too much difficulty. She is now back to her old self, thoroughly enjoying her work and getting results from her new students. This lady had courage and was able to face her tormentor with an outwardly confident and assertive attitude.

Here is another true example:

> Mr Y is an IT manager in a large law practice. He often works unsociable hours to access the system when it is not in use. This is not a problem for him as he is single with no family responsibilities, and is happy to work evenings and weekends. He has been with the company for ten years, and taking time off in lieu has never been a problem. There has been give and take. Recently one of his colleagues has been appointed office manager, a role which in terms of status is on a par with Mr Y's job. Mr Y is not accountable to the office manager, but to one of the senior partners.
>
> However, the office manager decides that he is going to take charge and in essence starts to throw his weight about, demanding written requests not only for holidays but for time off. Mr Y is a bit irritated, but he is not the sort to make a fuss and complies. As time goes on it becomes evident that Mr Y's requests for time off are more often than not refused. He asks his colleagues if they are experiencing the same problems – they say no. The difference between them and Mr Y is that they challenge the office manager rather than accept it. However, their style is much more abrasive than Mr Y feels comfortable with.
>
> Initially he believes that there is something wrong with him, and feels that perhaps he is being unreasonable. He discusses the problem with the head of personnel, who is sympathetic and has had her suspicions that the office manager wasn't using fair tactics. She gives Mr Y some assertiveness strategies which help him to stand up to the office manager, and with Mr Y's permission speaks to

the senior partner. He is unaware of the problem, particularly since the office manager has cleverly ingratiated himself with the senior partner. Luckily the senior partner trusts the judgement of the personnel manager and agrees to authorize a culture survey in the organization.

At the time of writing this manual the survey is being prepared. In the meantime Mr Y has sorted out his particular difficulty. It will be interesting to see whether his is an isolated case or not.

The point of these examples is that insignificant incidents on their own hardly seem worth noting, it is only when seen in the context of a build-up over a period of time that the total impact of bullying can be appreciated. Mrs X decided that the best course of action for her was to leave, but this is not always possible or advisable. Mr Y's case was different and he managed to address the problem successfully. If you need to keep your job then you need to marshal evidence and support to enhance your case.

If your organization has an anti-bullying policy in place then it is useful to look at the procedure. Familiarize yourself with the process and discuss it with the person in whom you have confided. You may decide that you are not yet ready to confront the bully or for someone else to do this on your behalf. If this is the case there are other things you can do.

Read the material in the toolkit which deals with behaviour (see Tools 1 and 2), so that you understand what is happening. You will also find Chapter 1 'Why people bully and how to understand the problem' helpful. Again, discuss this with your supporter. This will give you insight, but knowing why it is happening doesn't necessarily help you to deal with it. To do this you need to understand how you are reacting to the bullying and why. If you complete the 'Handling Aggression' questionnaire (see Tool 6 in the toolkit, page 94) you will become more aware of your own coping strategies. These may work to some degree, but there could be other, more productive ways of managing the situation. The results of the questionnaire will help you to select techniques which are appropriate for you.

You can work alone or with your supporter. It is often more productive to have someone guiding you through this because you may need a boost when your energy levels flag or you become dispirited if things don't always go to plan. Here are some pointers which will help you:

- Be systematic – work out what strategy you are going to use and stick with it for a defined period of time, say a month. Don't chop and change, it takes time for new behaviours to establish and become automatic.

- Monitor your performance – if you are monitoring how you feel emotionally about a situation, rate how you feel after an encounter with the bully. Are your anxiety levels still 10 out of 10, or not quite so high? Use the behaviour diary to record what happens (see Tool 19 in the toolkit) and look at your progress over time.

- Be realistic – if you have been struggling to deal with a bully and you have little confidence in yourself, the situation won't change overnight. Don't be too hard on yourself and take things one step at a time.

- Reward yourself – when things start to improve, give yourself a pat on the back. Treat yourself to something nice – a soothing massage, a trip to the cinema or a nice meal. It is important to look after yourself in this way.

As you start to build your confidence levels, you may feel more able to tackle the bully. What you may find is that because you are standing up to them and are no longer an easy target, they lose interest in you and move on. This may well solve your problem but it doesn't stop the bully.

Bullies are more likely to flourish in a culture which is either ruthless or hostile or which is *laissez faire*, where people choose to ignore what is going on and minimize or excuse bad behaviour. With an efficient anti-bullying policy in place in an organization, unacceptable behaviour will die out.

SUMMARY

This chapter has addressed some practical ways in which individuals can tackle the problem of bullying. However, in the toolkit which follows, even more specific anti-bullying strategies and techniques are introduced.

Part II
The Toolkit

Introduction to Part II

This toolkit is designed to help managers and individuals to cope with bullying at work. It is a practical resource and can be used in a variety of settings in a number of different ways.

The toolkit is divided into the following three chapters:

6 Models of behaviour – models for understanding and changing behaviour.
7 Understanding behaviour – tools for analysing problems.
8 Dealing with behaviour – tools to create more constructive behaviour.

MODELS OF BEHAVIOUR

There are five models based on psychological theory, which help to understand why people behave as they do. These models are explained in a straightforward way and give pointers for changing behaviour.

UNDERSTANDING BEHAVIOUR

It is important if something is going wrong in an organization, or if departments and individuals are experiencing problems, that these problems are tackled in a systematic and structured way. This section will help you to analyse exactly what is happening. From this you will be able to identify which of the tools in Chapter 8 (Dealing with Behaviour) are appropriate.

DEALING WITH BEHAVIOUR

These are the 'hands on' tools which will help to change behaviour. They can be used by managers working with their staff, or by individuals. The range of tools described here have their origins in training and therapy techniques. I have personally used all of them over the years with my clients and know that they work.

The toolkit matrix which follows gives you all the models and tools at a glance, so that you can select which you feel are most appropriate to your situation and circumstances.

The toolkit matrix

MODELS OF BEHAVIOUR

Tools – Models of behaviour	Purpose	Uses
1. Basic Behaviour Model (ABC)	To understand that all behaviour has a 'pay off', and we learn to behave in certain ways to achieve what we want.	To develop more constructive behaviour in individuals and groups by focusing on the reinforcement of positive behaviour.
2. Cognitive Behaviour Model	To understand that our behaviour is also driven by our past experiences, and that we can only change someone else's behaviour by changing our own.	To challenge existing thinking and judge whether those beliefs which drive our behaviour are productive or not.
3. Transactional Analysis Model	To understand that what we say (and how we say it) triggers a response in others – which can be productive or non-productive.	To apply the model to our interactions with others by being aware that certain words and phrases, and how they are spoken, will hook into our own beliefs. We can, however, choose to defuse a situation, rather than allow it to escalate.
4. OK Corral Model	The four behaviour scenarios – 'I'm OK, you're not OK' – 'I'm not OK, you're not OK' – 'I'm not OK, you're OK' and 'I'm OK, you're OK' gives us insight into how we value ourselves and others.	To help analyse the behaviour of individuals and groups/organizations to determine whether individuals are more likely to be bullies or victims. Also useful for examining the culture of an organization.
5. PUCA Model	The model helps to determine whether our behaviour is co-operative or unco-operative, assertive or passive.	The PUCA model defines what we need to do to develop assertive and co-operative behaviour. Used in conjunction with the Handling Aggression Questionnaire (Tool 6) it can guide managers to help their staff.

UNDERSTANDING BEHAVIOUR

Tools – Understanding behaviour	Purpose	Uses
6. Handling Aggression and Confrontational Situations Questionnaire	To analyse how you react and behave when faced with aggressive and intimidating behaviour.	For use with individuals or groups. The analysis will tell you whether you avoid confrontation, 'give as good as you get' and respond aggressively yourself, try to smooth things over or deal with aggression in a confident, assertive manner.
7. Locus of Control Questionnaire	To analyse whether individuals accept responsibility for their actions or blame others.	For use with individuals when trying to help them understand their behaviour. Will pinpoint which tools are appropriate in Chapter 8 of the toolkit.
8. Analyse your Behaviour Questionnaire	To analyse whether you are (or are in danger of becoming) a bully.	For use with anyone accused of bullying tactics. Can be used as a development tool for goal setting, and/or as part of the appraisal process.
9. Organizational Bullying Questionnaire	To analyse collective behaviour or corporate culture.	The results will tell you if there is a problem and the severity of it. There are also pointers as to what you should do.
10. Staff Survey on Bullying	A simple survey which can be distributed anonymously to gauge the extent of bullying in the organization.	Can be used to collect evidence towards pushing for an anti-bullying policy. Can also be used at a later date to check out whether policies are making a difference, that is, to draw comparisons.

DEALING WITH BEHAVIOUR

Tools – Dealing with behaviour	Purpose	Uses
11. Scripting	A technique used in assertiveness training to help people prepare for situations they find difficult to handle.	For individuals whose behaviour is either passive or aggressive (see Tool 1 for analysis). It will give them strategies for behaving more effectively.
12. Rehearsal	Another assertiveness technique which helps individuals to practise their skills.	As above for uses of Scripting.
13. Broken Record	How to get a point across in a measured way. Yet another assertiveness tool.	As above for uses of Scripting.
14. Saying 'No'	To ensure that an individual is not 'put upon' and takes on something which is not their responsibility.	Helping people to define their boundaries without feeling guilty. Can be used in conjunction with Tool 2 (Locus of Control).
15. Active Listening	To enable individuals to get the most out of their interaction with others.	Particularly useful for those who use bullying tactics. It will help them to see the value of really listening to people.
16. Anger Reduction	To enable individuals to deal with their anger more constructively than perhaps aiming it at others.	For anyone who has a tendency to be volatile or on a short fuse.
17. Challenging and Changing Thinking	To look at belief systems and work out whether they are appropriate or outmoded. If they no longer have credence, then to challenge and change them.	For individuals whose behaviour is inappropriate (whether passive or unco-operative). This tool can be used with Tool 19 (Harnessing Emotional Intelligence).
18. Confidence Boosters	Contains exercises and strategies to improve confidence and self-esteem.	Can be used as self-help strategies or with a manager, supporter or counsellor helping the individual concerned.
19. Harnessing Emotional Intelligence	To provide strategies for improving social skills and helping individuals to self-regulate their behaviour.	Individuals can use these techniques by themselves or with the guidance of another. The social skills are particularly useful for helping those who use bullying tactics.
20. Making an Action Plan	To draw upon the various techniques and strategies given in the toolkit and create an individual plan which is unique to that individual and which can be revised and amended.	To help individuals maintain impetus when they decide that they are going to tackle their problems.
21. Relaxation Techniques	A handful of exercises to help release tensions and promote a sense of calm and well-being.	For anyone who is feeling stressed and low as a result of being bullied or dealing with bullying (in a managerial sense).
22. Making a Buddy	To use an experienced member of staff to support and encourage more vulnerable employees.	For anyone who is new to an organization or has experienced problems.

Chapter 6
Models of behaviour

In this chapter you will find the following tools:

- Tool 1: Basic Behaviour Model (ABC)
- Tool 2: Cognitive Behaviour Model
- Tool 3: Transactional Analysis Model
- Tool 4: OK Corral Model
- Tool 5: PUCA Model.

These theoretical models help us to understand why we behave as we do. When we are trying to encourage more positive or constructive behaviour in the workplace, it is important to understand how difficult behaviour is perpetuated, often inadvertently, by the things we do and say.

The purpose of including these models in the toolkit is to help you to apply and use them on a day-to-day basis. You will be able to respond to others in a way that will lead and encourage them to interact with you in a positive way.

You will be able to:

- appreciate that all behaviour has a 'pay off', and this can lead to positive or negative outcomes
- understand that our belief systems (what we hold to be true about ourselves or others) affect our attitudes – which in turn govern our behaviour
- understand that if our belief systems are flawed, our behaviour will be inappropriate
- realize that you can only change someone else's behaviour by changing your own
- apply the principles of transactional analysis to your interactions with others, which will enable you to respond more appropriately to intimidating and bullying behaviour
- work out if you tend to behave passively or aggressively towards others, especially in difficult situations
- realize that you might be helping to perpetrate someone's bullying behaviour by the way you react to them.

TOOL 1: BASIC BEHAVIOUR MODEL (ABC)

Early learning theorists used a very simple model to explain behaviour (see Figure 6.1).

Figure 6.1 Basic behaviour model

$$\text{Stimulus} \Rightarrow \Rightarrow \Rightarrow \Rightarrow \text{Response}$$

In other words, behaviour (whether that be human or animal) can be seen to be a reaction to an event, a trigger or a set of circumstances. Later, theorists took this explanation a stage further to incorporate a consequence to the behaviour, and this model became known as the ABC model (see Figure 6.2).

Figure 6.2 ABC model

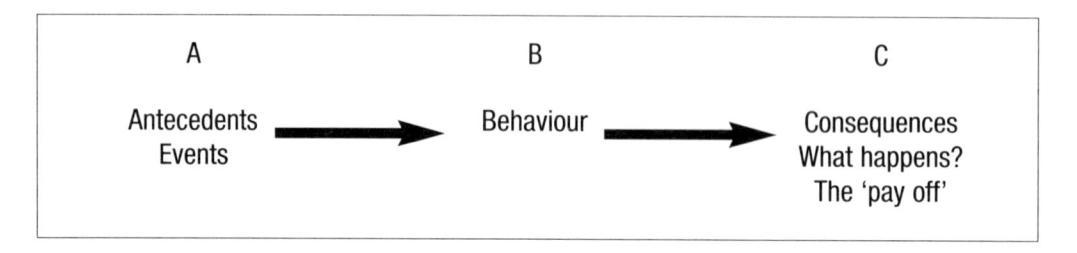

A	B	C
Antecedents Events	→ Behaviour →	Consequences What happens? The 'pay off'

A – The antecedents – what goes on before the trigger or event.

B – The behaviour – what is observable, what the person actually does.

C – The consequences – the pay off for behaving in a certain way.

The consequences aspect is important because it drives the behaviour. Here is a simple example:

> A young mum is pushing her toddler round the supermarket in a trolley. He sees some sweets that he wants, mum says 'no' but he starts to scream and throw himself about. Mum is so embarrassed and upset that she gives in and hands him the sweets. The child stops crying and is content.

Does this sound familiar?

What is happening in ABC terms?

A – The trigger	The child sees the sweets.
B – The behaviour	The child screams and has a tantrum.
C – The consequences	Mum gives him the sweets.

What will happen on the next shopping trip? You've guessed it! The child has learned that the pay off to behaving in this way is that he gets what he wants, and so he will do it again. It is not much different to an adult throwing a wobbler to get his or her own way. It happens all the time.

Of course the longer term consequences are somewhat different. The child learns that obnoxious behaviour gets results and unless it is challenged, this behaviour or something similar, will continue into adult life. However, they may find that others give them a wide berth, or they don't have many friends – which means that the behaviour in the long term will be counter productive.

In a sense the example given shows a negative pay off, but this isn't always the case. In a work situation, for example, if someone is working conscientiously and this behaviour is commented on and appreciated by others they will continue to do it. The pay off here is that 'it makes me feel good, so I'll carry on'.

USING THE BASIC BEHAVIOUR MODEL

The basic behaviour or ABC model can help you to motivate your staff and develop more productive behaviour. You can make sure that the 'pay offs' are what you want. Comment on 'good' behaviour, that is, when things are going well, and resist the urge to nag at every misdemeanour. Thank people for working well together, completing a good piece of work, dealing with a difficult customer or putting in the extra effort to get a rushed job completed on time. You will be surprised at how well this works. The 'pay off' for staff is that they will feel valued and noticed.

TOOL 2: COGNITIVE BEHAVIOUR MODEL

This is a more sophisticated development of the ABC model because it includes thinking. The theory behind this model is that we do not behave or respond to a situation without some thought having gone into it – whether conscious or unconscious.

Our thinking is affected by lots of different things. It may be beliefs that we hold which affect our attitude. For example:

> 'You have to work hard in this life, nothing comes free. If you don't put 120% in all the time you're never going to get anywhere.'

> 'You can't trust small people, they always have a Hitler complex.'

These beliefs do not have to be based on logic and reason – in many instances they are illogical, irrational and without foundation.

Our thinking may be affected by our personality type. We may be pessimistic or optimistic by nature, quick to make decisions or more measured in our approach, hot tempered or placid. Our own psychological traits will influence our thinking and therefore how we behave.

Thinking can also be affected by our life experiences (as explained by social learning theory described in Chapter 1). A small child may have learned to manipulate others by adopting a weak, vulnerable persona. The subconscious thinking as an adult would be:

> 'I can get people to do what I want if I behave in a feeble and dependent way.'

It may be that an individual has learned in the past that others always get the better of them in arguments or debates, and that they are not good at thinking on their feet. If this is the case they will avoid getting into this sort of situation. Their subconscious thinking would be:

> 'I'm not good at stating my case, so I'm going to avoid getting into any discussion about this.'

Or it might be:

> 'Let them get on with it, anything for a quiet life.'

All our thoughts or cognitions are driven by what we believe, have experienced or the type of people we are. These in turn drive our behaviour, which can be acceptable or unacceptable.

As with the ABC model of behaviour, the consequences or pay off feed back into the behaviour pattern. If we are rewarded for bad behaviour – as in the earlier example of the child in the supermarket – we continue to do it. However, if that behaviour is disapproved of or becomes non-productive it dies out. In psychological terms it is extinguished.

Figures 6.3, 6.4 and 6.5 explain the cognitive behaviour model.

Figure 6.3 Cognitive behaviour model

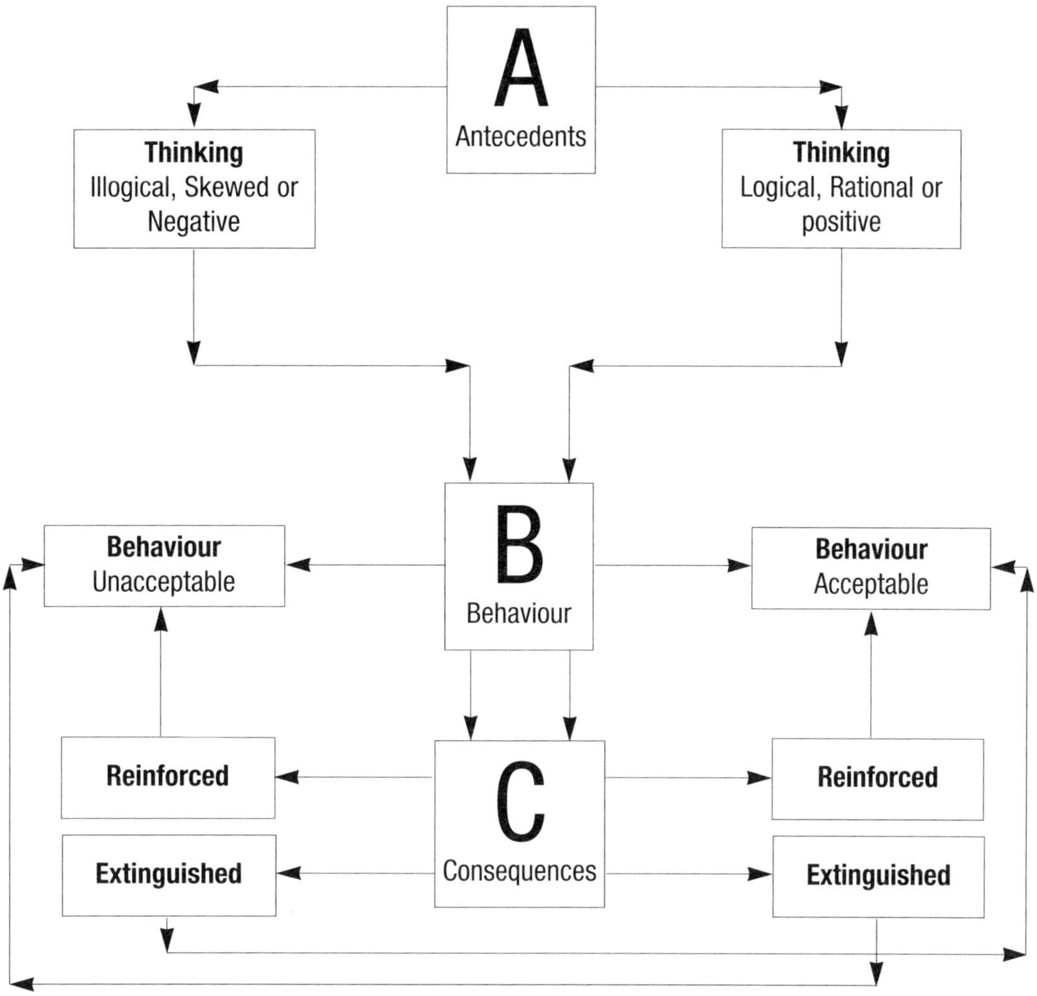

Elaine Douglas © 1997

SUB MODEL A

If our thinking is illogical, skewed or negative, we behave in an unacceptable way. This does not necessarily have to be 'bad' behaviour, but it is behaviour which in the long term is not productive or helpful. If this behaviour is reinforced, that is, the feedback we get from others confirms to us that it is OK to behave like this, then we will carry on. However, if the feedback tells us that this behaviour is disapproved of or not acceptable, we will change it to more acceptable behaviour.

Figure 6.4 Cognitive behaviour model – sub model A

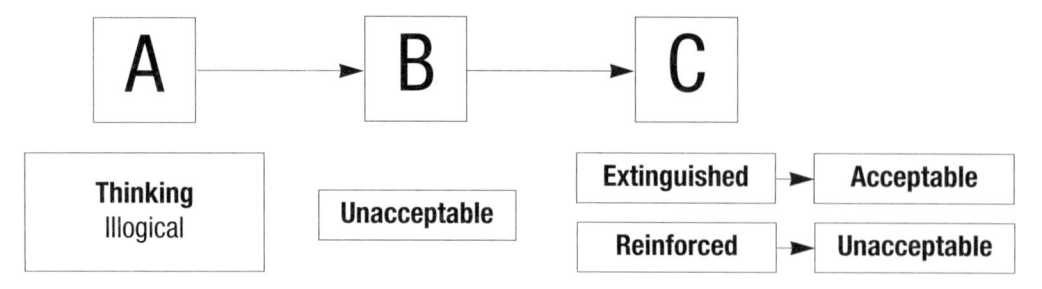

```
    A  →  B  →  C

Thinking        Extinguished → Acceptable
Illogical   Unacceptable
                Reinforced  → Unacceptable
```

Elaine Douglas © 1997

SUB MODEL B

If our thinking is logical, rational and positive we will behave in an acceptable way. If we get positive feedback from others we will continue to do so. However, if our 'good' behaviour is not acknowledged or is seen not to fit in to the culture of the organization or environment we are in, it will diminish. In other words, good behaviour can be extinguished, just as easily as bad if the conditions are detrimental.

Figure 6.5 Cognitive behaviour model – sub model B

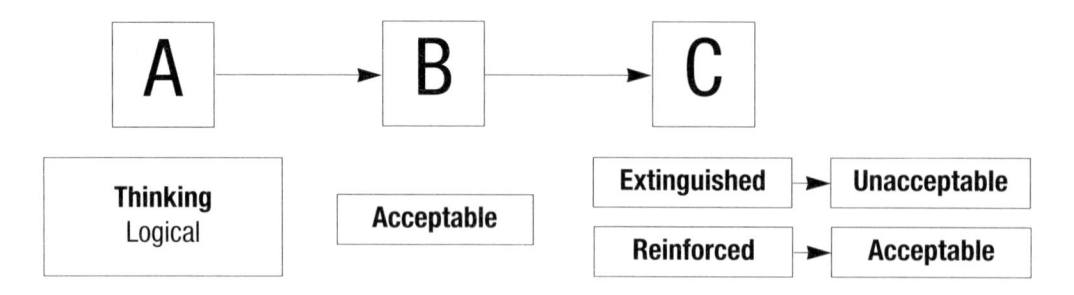

```
    A  →  B  →  C

Thinking        Extinguished → Unacceptable
Logical    Acceptable
                Reinforced  → Acceptable
```

Elaine Douglas © 1997

Let us take a case in point to illustrate how unacceptable behaviour can change.

A CASE STUDY

Alan is head of the administration department. He believes that the only way to get people to work is to be on their backs constantly. To this end he nags, harasses and shouts at his team of four women.

They are intimidated by him but are frightened or unwilling to stand up for themselves. They do their work, but without enthusiasm and generally try to avoid him. If he rants and raves there is a flurry of activity – but also a lot of dispirited, disaffected workers.

Alan thinks his behaviour achieves results. It is obvious! The more he shouts, the more they do – at least until the heat is off. By behaving in a passive manner his team are unwittingly helping to perpetuate the problem. Alan is not going to change his behaviour because he believes it to be effective. In addition, their reaction to his behaviour will reinforce his belief that workers are inherently lazy and need to be jumped on.

Let's introduce some changes.

Sally, one of the team, has worked for Alan for two years. She has put up with his bullying tactics all this time because she needed the money. However, her husband has just been promoted at his place of work. Sally realizes that she no longer needs the money as much as she used to, and decides that she's not going to suffer the situation any longer.

The next time Alan blows up she challenges him, not confrontationally, but nevertheless standing her ground. She tells him how his behaviour makes her feel and the effect it has on all of them. The others gain confidence from her stance and support her. Alan is outraged. Sally is not put off and remains calm, stating that they will not work for him if he continues to behave in this way.

To cut a long story short – these things never happen overnight – Alan realizes that he's getting nowhere and begrudgingly (at first) he starts to calm down. He begins to ask for things to be done, rather than order people around. He begins to realize that if he is reasonable with them, they will be reasonable with him.

Here is the key:

You can only change someone else's behaviour by changing your own.

USING THE COGNITIVE BEHAVIOUR MODEL

This model can help you to understand your own behaviour, and that of others. Possibly the best example to use in terms of addressing bullying behaviour is the belief that many managers feel that they have to demonstrate strong management. There is nothing wrong with being a strong manager, as long as this is not translated into ordering people around and disregarding their feelings and opinions. Some managers erroneously believe that this is the only way to get things done. It often stems from lack of training in management skills and emulating the behaviour of senior managers. However, these role models are basically flawed.

Think about how your behaviour is impacting on others. Are you really getting the best out of them if you shout and bawl? Think of more productive ways to achieve results. Put yourself in their shoes – would you respond well to these sorts of bullying tactics? If you start to change your behaviour towards others, they will respond to you.

TOOL 3: TRANSACTIONAL ANALYSIS MODEL

Transactional analysis comes from a theory of personality pioneered by Eric Berne in the early 1970s (see Further reading and useful contacts, page 183). The theory was originally used in a clinical setting, but was later applied in a wider context. It has proved to be extremely useful in explaining behaviour in organizations and families.

Berne suggests that the personality consists of three major parts, or ego states. These are Parent, Adult and Child. He proposes that as individuals we have a preference to operate in one of these states most of the time, although we can switch to other modes. The terms Parent, Adult and Child do not have anything to do with being a parent, adult or child. What he means is that we behave in a parental, adult or child-like way.

See Figure 6.6 for a representation of the three ego states.

Figure 6.6 Transactional analysis ego states

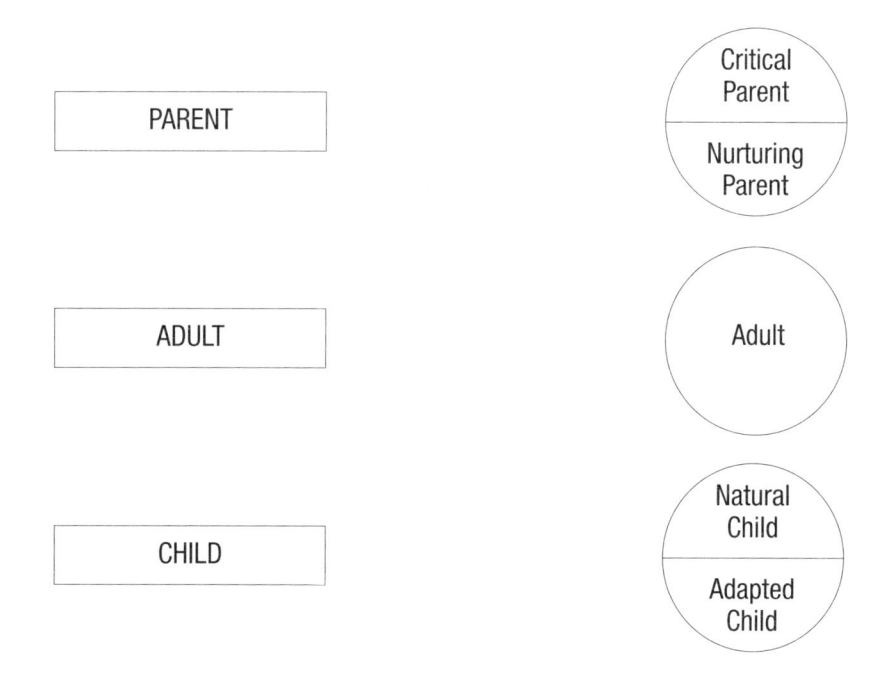

PARENT

The parent ego state is usually divided into two parts, the Critical Parent and the Nurturing Parent. The Critical Parent is perceived as being authoritarian, critical and inconsiderate of the feelings of others. Many managers can and do behave in this way, as do many actual parents with their own children. The Nurturing Parent is softer and more considerate and is concerned about the welfare of others. Again, some individuals in positions of responsibility operate in this way. However, the negative connotations of this nurturing mode of behaviour can be that it is too stifling, claustrophobic and ultimately debilitating.

A Critical Parent might say:

> 'These sales figures are absolutely atrocious, this company isn't paying you lot to sit on your backsides and do nothing. I want it sorted now.'

> 'I told you not to disturb me when I'm working on this project. Now get out and leave me alone.'

A Nurturing Parent might say:

> 'Do you really think you're up to this business trip? You know you always suffer from jet lag.'

> 'Don't work too hard, you'll wear yourself out.'

ADULT

The Adult ego state epitomizes logical and rational thinking. However, the down side is that it can sometimes appear quite clinical and cold. If you think of Data or Mr Spock in *Star Trek*, then you have some idea of the behaviour of someone operating in Adult mode – when it is taken to extremes. However, responding in Adult mode to someone who is not operating from a constructive ego state can defuse potential problems.

Someone in Adult mode might say:

> 'These figures are down on last month. We need to look at why this is and make a plan of action to rectify it.'

> (To a child) 'If you finish your dinner then we'll have some time to go down to the park and get an ice-cream on the way.'

CHILD

The Child state represents in some ways freer emotional responses. These can be positive or negative. The Child ego state is divided into two parts, the Natural Child and the Adapted Child. The Natural Child is free and spontaneous, full of fun and energy. The Adapted Child can either be sullen and rebellious or passive and withdrawn. Quite often the 'Child' response will happen when someone else is operating in Parent mode. It is not difficult to imagine someone using the authoritarian, bullying tactics of Critical Parent eliciting a response which is either:

- resentful, harbouring a grudge, wanting to get back at them, or
- tearful, distressed and retreating into a shell.

If the Natural Child comes out, the reaction to a bullying manager might be:

> 'Oh, to hell with him, let's go down the pub!'

If the Adapted Child kicks in, communication will not be constructive. However, the exuberant, energetic outlook of the Natural Child can often inject humour and perspective into a situation, and help to restore harmony.

LOOKING AT TRANSACTIONS

Transactions are basically units of behaviour which involve saying or doing something to someone else and them responding (or vice versa). For the purposes of this material, a transaction is verbal behaviour (but it can be non-verbal, for example fist shaking, finger wagging and pointing).

The following examples will help you to make sense of these interactions and help to minimize or eradicate the difficult behaviours of Critical Parent and Adapted Child.

Example 1

Example of a transaction between Adults:

> Person A: 'Can you tell me how to get to the newsagents?'
>
> Person B: 'Yes, straight on to the traffic lights and turn left.'

See Figure 6.7.

Figure 6.7 Transactions between Adults

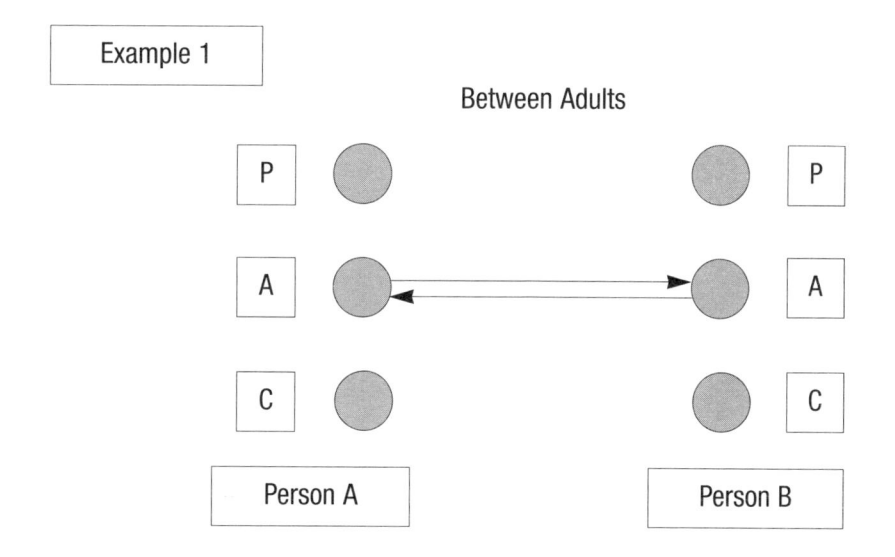

Example 2

Example of a transaction between Natural Child and Nurturing Parent:

> Person A: 'Can you help me find this reference book?'
>
> Person B: 'Of course I can, don't you worry about it at all, I'll get it for you.'

See Figure 6.8.

BULLYING IN THE WORKPLACE

Figure 6.8 Transactions between Natural Child and Nurturing Parent

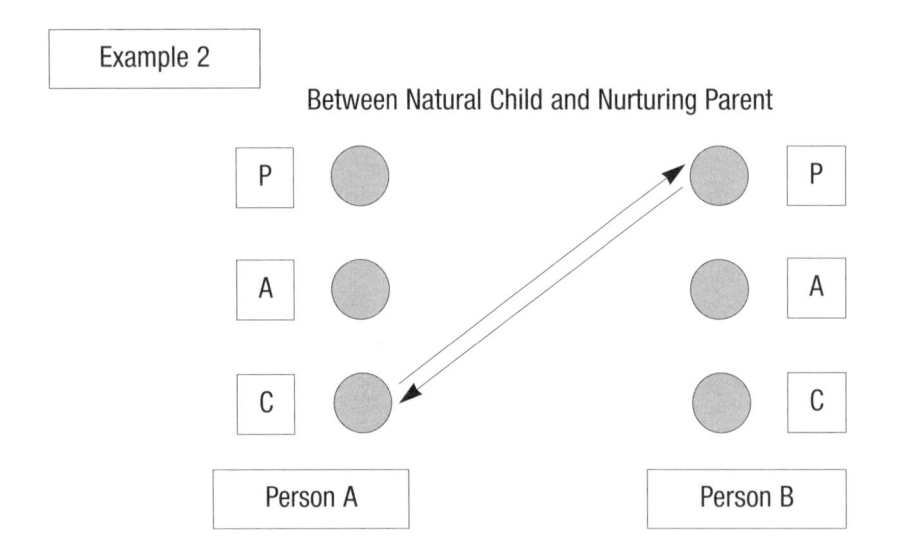

Example 2

Between Natural Child and Nurturing Parent

Person A   Person B

Example 3

Example of a transaction between Critical Parent and Critical Parent:

Person A: 'Move that box from over there, it's in the way.'

Person B: 'Don't tell me what to do, move it yourself.'

See Figure 6.9.

Figure 6.9 Transactions between Critical Parent and Critical Parent

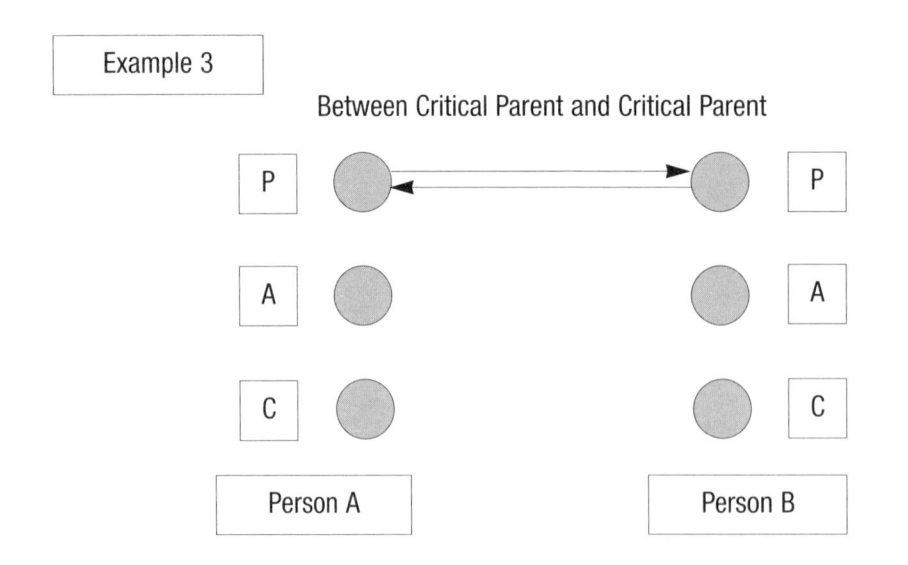

Example 3

Between Critical Parent and Critical Parent

Person A   Person B

Example 4

Example of a transaction between Adapted Child and Adapted Child:

Person A: 'Let's let Fred's tyres down, he's been a pain in the neck all week.'

Person B: 'Oh I don't think we should, what if he finds out?'

Can you see how Person A's statement or question leads to a response from Person B? These are just a few examples, but they illustrate the point that what we want to say (and how we say it) can 'hook into' the other person.

Look at the authoritarian, bossy statement from Person A in the third example:

'Move that box from over there, it's in the way.'

This rubs Person B up the wrong way and he or she responds in the same fashion.

'Don't tell me what to do, move it yourself.'

These types of interaction are called parallel, and will continue until they are 'crossed' by a response from another ego state.

Example 5

Example of a transaction between Critical Parent and Adapted Child:

Person A: 'Where are those papers I left on my desk? Someone's moved them again.'

Person B: 'There you go, blaming me as usual. You're always on at me.'

Person A: 'Well if the cap fits.'

Bossy Critical Parent 'hooks into' truculent Adapted Child, which in turn aggravates Critical Parent even more; hence the comment 'Well if the cap fits'.

There will never be a positive outcome to this unless one of them responds in a different way. In a revision of Example 5, Person B chooses not to respond in Adapted Child mode but in Adult mode.

The outcome would be different if this happened:

Person A: 'Where are those papers I left on my desk? Someone's moved them again.'

Person B: 'I think they're back in the filing cabinet.'

Person A: 'Oh right, thanks, I'll have a look.'

Person A starts to come down off his high horse and reply in a more measured way.

If this time Person A chooses to respond in an Adult way, the outcome would also be different.

Person A: 'Where are those papers I left on my desk? Someone's moved them again.'

Person B: 'There you go, blaming me as usual. You're always on at me.'

Person A: 'I'm not blaming you. I need them for a meeting and I'm running late.'

It is only through 'crossing' an interaction that you will break the pattern, which will lead to a more constructive outcome.

HOW TO USE TRANSACTIONAL ANALYSIS

If someone says something to you that you find offensive, belittling or rude or is said in a manner which patronizes you, try to put your Adult head on, for example:

> Critical Parent: 'That suggestion is absolute rubbish.'
>
> Adult: 'Can you explain why you've reached that conclusion? What evidence have you got to support that statement?'

You could also try to defuse the situation by injecting some humour into the proceedings by using a Natural Child response, for example:

> 'Hey wait a minute, this is me you're talking to, not your mother in law!'

Remember also the old adage – 'It aint what you say, it's the way that you say it.' Many unnecessary flare-ups occur when someone's intonation suggests Critical Parent or Adapted Child.

The most important thing is to try not to get into a head-to-head confrontation – as will happen if you respond in Critical Parent mode – or become petulant, difficult or tearful – as will happen if you respond to something like the above in Adapted Child mode. Neither of these responses will lead to productive behaviour or sort out the problem.

Think about the phrases that are often used these days:

> 'He knows which buttons to press.'
>
> 'She really winds me up.'

You are in charge of your own behaviour, and you will be 'wound up' only if you allow it to happen. Don't respond emotionally, and think before you say or do something. If you can give yourself that breathing space you will be amazed at the difference it makes.

Using these principles will help you to respond more appropriately to intimidating and bullying behaviour. You will be less likely to be 'put down' or 'put upon'. Look at Tools 11, 12 and 13, which look at Scripting, Rehearsal and Broken Record. They will help you to develop your repertoire of responses.

TOOL 4: OK CORRAL MODEL

There is another piece of theory from transactional analysis which is useful in understanding behaviour. The concept is concerned with whether or not someone is OK – meaning all right, valued as a person.

An OK person is in control of their life and their views and opinions are taken seriously. Conversely, if someone is not OK they are perceived as not being in control and their views and opinions are dismissed. This concept can be applied to oneself and to others.

This concept was originally devised by Franklin Ernst for use in psychotherapy. However, like that of transactional analysis it is now used much more broadly. There are four categories based on being (or not being) 'OK'.

I'M OK, YOU'RE NOT OK

If I'm OK then I have value as a person and my opinions and ideas matter. If you're not OK then you do not matter, your ideas and opinions don't count. In organizational terms, this approach leads to a 'hire and fire' mentality.

I'M NOT OK, YOU'RE NOT OK

In this situation no one knows what is going on and no one appears to be in control. It often shows itself in an organizational form in the type of office 'joke' stickers that read:

> 'You don't have to be mad to work here, but it helps!'

I'M NOT OK, YOU'RE OK

In many ways this is the reverse of I'm OK, you're not OK. Everyone else is fine and in control, but as a person you are not. When taken to extremes it can be characterized by taking the blame for everything – it's all my fault. A more common reaction is to withdraw or keep a low profile.

I'M OK, YOU'RE OK

In this position I'm of value and so are you. We are both in control of ourselves and the situation, and although we may not always agree with each other it does not mean that we don't value each other. This is the only position from which people can interact effectively.

Most of us operate in the 'I'm OK, you're OK' position most of the time. However, at times of stress or when problems or difficulties arise we tend to fall back into one of the other positions. The position we choose will depend on a number of things – personality, past experiences, the situation and so on. However, the commonality of the other three positions is that they are very unproductive in terms of creating good interpersonal interaction and relationships.

HOW TO USE THE OK CORRAL

Ernst's theory can give us insight into looking at how people behave with each other, and also how the organization seems to function. Ask yourself the following questions:

- Do senior managers in the organization appear aloof and distant from the workforce?
- Do they encourage a 'them and us' mentality?
- Do they appear to be dismissive of their staff?
- Do they ignore the opinions of others and/or stifle their creativity?

If you answer 'yes' to any of these questions then in Ernst's terms their attitude is 'I'm OK, you're not OK.' If this is the case then you seriously need to consider using the Organizational Bullying questionnaire (Tool 9) to find out the extent of the problem.

Furthermore, you need to set up an anti-bullying policy in the organization (see Chapter 2 on how to do this). If there is a policy in place, then it is not working. You will need to examine why this is the case and look closely at what is preventing it from being effective.

Let us have a look at what else might be happening. Consider these questions:

- Does your organization lack direction?
- Is there an absence of goals, objectives or a mission statement?
- Do people bumble along without clear job descriptions and responsibilities?
- Are you constantly 'fire-fighting' rather than being in control?
- Does everything seem to be chaotic?

If you answer 'yes' to any of these questions then your organization would appear to be displaying 'I'm not OK, you're not OK' characteristics. It is not necessarily the case that bullying tactics will be evident in the organization (which is definitely the case with 'I'm OK, you're not OK'), but the lack of structure and looseness of the organization could well produce a lot of pressure. If no one knows exactly what they should be doing and how they should be doing it, when will they know if they have achieved anything?

Pressure bullying can occur in this kind of environment – it tends to cascade down from the top. For example, shareholders may demand more returns on their investments which means there is a need for increased sales or manufacture of goods. The MD pushes the sales director and the operations director, who in turn pass it down the line. Unrealistic expectations can result, especially if no one really knows what is going on. It is easy to see how bullying could thrive.

If this sounds familiar to you then you need to get down to basics and consider forward planning, clear objectives for the company and well defined roles and responsibilities.

The instance of 'I'm not OK, you're OK' probably concerns individual rather than collective behaviour. Think about your colleagues (and yourself for that matter). Do any of these questions apply to you or any of your colleagues or staff?

- Do you automatically think it's your fault if something goes wrong at work?
- Do you take responsibility for things which 'belong' to someone else?
- Do you find it hard to say 'no'?
- Do you find yourself snowed under with work?

If you feel that these questions describe you (or a colleague), then one or two things may be happening. You are finding it difficult to set boundaries for yourself in terms of what you should and should not be taking on, and/or you are in danger of being an easy target for a bully. If this is the case you need to study this toolkit carefully, as there are lots of strategies which will help you. In particular, you need to get to the bottom of why you feel that 'you're not OK'. Sometimes it helps to consult a professional counsellor or psychologist if this really is a problem for you. However, if this doesn't appeal to you, test yourself on the Handling Aggression and Confrontational Situations Questionnaire (Tool 6), and look at the matrix at the beginning of the toolkit to pinpoint which strategies you feel would be most useful to you.

If you recognize these signs in a colleague, then talk to them. Support them and help them to implement the strategies given in the toolkit.

TOOL 5: PUCA MODEL Eda©1997

This model uses elements from Berne, Ernst and the conflict mode instrument proposed by Thomas Kilmann (see Further reading and useful contacts, page 183). It combines four types of behaviour – passive, unco-operative, co-operative and assertive, and it suggests that we should aspire to behave in a co-operative and assertive manner.

The PUCA model looks at four different types of behaviour, three of which are ultimately non-productive. These behaviour types are:

- unco-operative and passive
- unco-operative and assertive
- co-operative and passive
- co-operative and assertive.

These four behaviour types actually give us two continuums (see Figure 6.10).

Figure 6.10 PUCA model – the two continuums

Unco-operative ⇔⇔⇔ Co-operative

Passive ⇔⇔⇔ Assertive

UNCO-OPERATIVE AND PASSIVE

Behaviour in this dimension is characterized by withdrawing or avoiding a person or situation. The individual does not engage; he or she removes themselves from any interaction which may lead to conflict or confrontation. Their motto could be 'Leave me out of it, it's not my problem!'

UNCO-OPERATIVE AND ASSERTIVE

Behaviour in this dimension is characterized by being forceful and confrontational. The individual speaks his or her mind, but does not listen to the other person. They wish to push their opinions, ideas and so on at the expense of the other person's views and in so doing are unlikely to reach agreement. This behaviour typifies the bully.

CO-OPERATIVE AND PASSIVE

This behaviour is represented by accommodating others and keeping the peace. Individuals do not disengage as in the unco-operative/passive dimension but tend to smooth things over and appease others. Their motto could be 'Anything for a quiet life.'

CO-OPERATIVE AND ASSERTIVE

This behaviour is evidenced by collaboration and joint problem-solving. Individuals are aware of their own needs and those of others. They actively seek opportunities to work things out with colleagues. In Ernst terms this is 'I'm OK, you're OK.'

Of the four dimensions, it becomes apparent that three are maladaptive. That is to say that they may well work in the short term, but in the long run they are not constructive. For example:

- **Avoiding** – this means that there aren't any confrontations, but nothing is accomplished. Anything that does get done is done without consultation, to everybody's irritation.
- **Competing** – bullying tactics will work if others operate in a passive, co-operative style, but what are the long-term consequences?
- **Accommodating** – perpetuates the problem and runs the risk of individuals moving into an unco-operative mode because they are tired of constantly massaging other people's egos.

For people to get on with each other, decisions to be made and problems to be solved, they must display co-operative, assertive behaviour, i.e. collaborating. See Figure 6.11.

Figure 6.11 PUCA model

Unco-operative/Assertive	Co-operative/Assertive
Competing	**Collaborating**
Confrontational Pushy Will not listen Typifies the bully	Aware of others' needs Actively seek opportunities to work with others
Avoiding	**Accommodating**
Withdrawing Will not engage in conflict or confrontation	Keep the peace Appease others Anything for a quiet life
Unco-operative/Passive	**Co-operative/Passive**

Chapter 7
Understanding behaviour

In this chapter you will find the following tools:

- Tool 6: Handling Aggression and Confrontational Situations Questionnaire
- Tool 7: Locus of Control Questionnaire
- Tool 8: Analyse your Behaviour Questionnaire
- Tool 9: Organizational Bullying Questionnaire
- Tool 10: Staff Survey on Bullying.

Using these tools will help you to identify the problem(s) more specifically. Each tool is described in detail, with guidance as to how and when to use it. A summary of what will be achieved is given under the heading 'outcomes', as well as advice on what to do next.

TOOL 6: HANDLING AGGRESSION AND CONFRONTATIONAL SITUATIONS QUESTIONNAIRE

PURPOSE

This questionnaire has been designed to analyse how individuals react to aggression and confrontational situations.

SITUATION

The questionnaire can be used for self-development, and for managers to use with their staff or professionals with their clients.

DESCRIPTION

The questionnaire is made up of 44 questions. Individuals should select which word (usually, sometimes or rarely) applies to them and to tick the appropriate box.

The information gleaned from this questionnaire will identify the following four behaviour types:

1. You tend to avoid confrontation and, therefore, perhaps get taken advantage of. Behaving in a passive way means that it is probably difficult for you to stand up for yourself.
2. You respond to confrontation with confrontation. If you have a tendency to 'give as good as you get', then your relationships with colleagues may well suffer. You may even be regarded as being intimidating and difficult.
3. You are one of life's peacemakers and you try hard to smooth things over because you dislike upset. In many ways this is an admirable quality, but there may well come a point when you feel resentful that you always seem to be massaging someone's ego.
4. You don't shy away from confrontation, but face it in an assertive and confident manner. This is the only type of behaviour which will lead to 'win–win' situations, and is what we need to strive to attain.

METHOD

This is a self-reporting questionnaire and as such could be open to abuse. When completing it, people need to be honest with themselves. They should not answer the questions as they think they would like to behave, or as they think they ought to behave. They need to answer truthfully about what they actually do.

If you are a manager using the questionnaire as a development tool with a member of staff, or as part of helping victims of bullying or bullies themselves, you might want to use the following script:

'This questionnaire is designed to identify how you respond in a conflict situation or to confrontation. I/we would like you to answer as honestly and fully as you can. This will enable me/us to help you in the most productive way possible. I/we will not make judgements about your responses as the most important thing is to identify how you react and not dwell on individual answers.'

However, experience of using this material does seem to suggest that most people *believe* that they behave in a co-operative and assertive way for the majority of the time. Consequently, their highest score tends to be in the optimum co-operative/assertive dimension.

It may be the case that they do usually deal with situations in a constructive way, and it is perhaps something out of the ordinary which triggers off less desirable responses. However, there may be a little bit of wishful thinking, and a tendency to look at things through rose-coloured glasses.

It is helpful if you suspect that this may be the case to look at the next highest score. This may well give you a truer picture of what is happening. It will certainly help you to understand more clearly how disagreements and problems remain unresolved because of specific types of behaviour and responses.

The questionnaire is not timed, and individuals should be given as much time as they need. Reassure them that the information is confidential and to be used only for the purpose of resolving the problem.

Handling Aggression and Confrontational Situations Questionnaire

Page 1 of 3

A = Usually   B = Sometimes   C = Rarely

During a confrontation with a colleague do you...   **A   B   C**

1. Discuss the issue with the individual or those involved?

2. Quietly not co-operate?

3. Try to get even?

4. Make a joke about the whole thing?

5. Go to your supervisor or someone higher up for support or advice?

6. Don't talk to the aggressor?

7. Try to convince the other person of your point of view?

8. Try to smooth things over?

9. Try and defuse their anger?

10. Get the person to leave?

11. Make excuses to get away as quickly as possible?

12. Talk constructively to co-workers/colleagues?

13. Take a drink or a pill afterwards?

14. Form alliances against the aggressor?

15. Accept the conflict?

16. Try to see the other person's point of view whilst holding your own opinion?

17. Ignore the conflict?

18. Shout a lot during the interaction?

Page 2 of 3

	A	B	C
19. Do what the other person says?	☐	☐	☐
20. Speak calmly without losing your temper?	☐	☐	☐
21. Ask for a transfer?	☐	☐	☐
22. Mop up the trail of destruction?	☐	☐	☐
23. Listen carefully to what's being said without expressing your own views?	☐	☐	☐
24. Avoid contact with that person?	☐	☐	☐
25. Push or punch the other person?	☐	☐	☐
26. Take on responsibility for the problem whether it is yours or not?	☐	☐	☐
27. Engage in active listening?	☐	☐	☐
28. Avoid eye contact during the interaction?	☐	☐	☐
29. Throw things?	☐	☐	☐
30. Try not to make waves?	☐	☐	☐
31. Use non-threatening body language?	☐	☐	☐
32. Turn your body or head away during the interaction?	☐	☐	☐
33. Keep your head down and get on with it?	☐	☐	☐
34. Talk constructively to friends about it?	☐	☐	☐
35. Cry or become distressed?	☐	☐	☐
36. Talk behind their back?	☐	☐	☐
37. Take the flack?	☐	☐	☐
38. State your case whilst accepting theirs?	☐	☐	☐

Page 3 of 3

	A	B	C
39. Take time off?	☐	☐	☐
40. Sabotage the aggressor's efforts?	☐	☐	☐
41. Keep the peace, possibly at a cost to yourself?	☐	☐	☐
42. Use your authority to gain control?	☐	☐	☐
43. Answer in monosyllables or not at all?	☐	☐	☐
44. Try to accommodate everyone?	☐	☐	☐

Scoring the Handling Aggression and Confrontational Situations Questionnaire

Page 1 of 2

a) On the following questions:

1, 5, 9, 12, 16, 20, 23, 27, 31, 34 and 38

Score
- 2 points for **Usually**
- 1 point for **Sometimes**
- 0 points for **Rarely**

Put your total in here:

[ ]   Box A

b) On the following questions:

4, 8, 15, 19, 22, 26, 30, 33, 37, 41 and 44

Score
- 2 points for **Usually**
- 1 point for **Sometimes**
- 0 points for **Rarely**

Put your total in here:

[ ]   Box B

c) On the following questions:

3, 7, 10, 14, 18, 21, 25, 29, 36, 40 and 42

Score
- 2 points for **Usually**
- 1 point for **Sometimes**
- 0 points for **Rarely**

Put your total in here:

[ ]   Box C

Page 2 of 2

d) On the following questions:

2, 6, 11, 13, 17, 24, 28, 32, 35, 39 and 43

Score
2 points for **Usually**
1 point for **Sometimes**
0 points for **Rarely**

Put your total in here:

☐ Box D

Transfer your scores here.

☐ Box A = Co-operative/Assertive

☐ Box B = Co-operative/Passive

☐ Box C = Unco-operative/Assertive

☐ Box D = Unco-operative/Assertive

Your two highest scores will indicate which behaviours you tend to adopt in confrontational situations.

Your two lowest scores will indicate which behaviours you are least likely to adopt in confrontational situations.

UNDERSTANDING THE RESULTS AND GIVING FEEDBACK – GUIDANCE FOR MANAGERS AND PROFESSIONALS

Now you have the scores and an analysis as to how an individual tends to respond to aggression. It may be that they do not fall into one clear behaviour category. This is fine. It means that he or she has a range of strategies to deal with a number of eventualities. However, if most of their responses fall into the categories of unco-operative/passive, unco-operative/assertive or co-operative/passive it means that although they may have a wide ranging repertoire, none of it is effective. They need to achieve a high score in the co-operative/assertive mode to be successful at dealing with conflict.

If there is a distribution over all four categories, with more or less equal weighting, then you need to check what is going on. It is unusual for someone who behaves in a constructive way (that is, assertive and co-operative) to use the other styles equally. A mixture of responses in other categories is not significant, as long as the assertive/co-operative is the highest. However, high scores in any of the other three modes could create problems. It may well mean that in times of stress or pressure the individual will operate by becoming stroppy, withdrawing or trying to please everyone. When discussing the results with your client or colleague, you need to discover whether this is the case.

You may get a profile which does not seem to fit the individual concerned, or appears to conflict with the information you have been given. If this is the case, you may need to do some digging!

Here's what to do:

1. Explain to the individual concerned that you are puzzled by the profile. They may be able to tell you why there are discrepancies or inconsistencies. Talk to them – they may just have had a really bad day when they filled in the questionnaire, and the results are skewed.
2. If this doesn't work or proves inconclusive, explain to the individual that you need to speak to someone who knows them well, to try and get a rounded picture. Be direct about this, it will create more problems if you go behind their back.
3. You may be enlightened by just talking to one of their colleagues. However, you may want to ask that colleague to complete the questionnaire on behalf of the person you are working with, focusing on how they feel the individual would behave.
4. Look at the two sets of scores. What are the differences, what are the similarities? Use this as a basis for discussion with the person you're working with. If they haven't been entirely honest with you or themselves, it will come out.

A word of caution here. This exercise must be done sensitively and with empathy and understanding towards the individual. If you are judgemental or apportion blame you will make things worse. If you are unsure as to whether you can do this, speak to someone in your organization who has the necessary skills. If this is not possible you may need to refer the case on to a consulting psychologist or experienced counsellor.

You should explain to individuals that it is better that they know and understand their own capabilities and breadth of skills (and when these are not enough for a really serious problem) than to blunder on regardless.

OUTCOMES

From your investigations, you will have a clear idea of the behaviours you as an individual or your member of staff use when faced with confrontation. If there is room for modification or development look at the matrix at the beginning of the toolkit (see pages 70–72) to find out which tools are relevant to your situation. Decide what you are going to do to change your behaviour, and if it is helpful use the action plan (see Tool 20) to get you started.

TOOL 7: LOCUS OF CONTROL QUESTIONNAIRE

PURPOSE

This questionnaire is designed to look at whether individuals are happy to accept responsibility for their actions, or tend to blame others and find fault in what other people do.

The concept of locus of control is described fully so that you will be able to understand how it works, and what application it can have in the workplace.

SITUATION

The questionnaire is an excellent tool to use if and when allegations have been made about bullying. In particular, it can be used by managers who are trying to work with those accused of bullying.

DESCRIPTION

There are some situations where individuals need to accept and acknowledge their responsibility. For example, if you are looking after a young child it is your responsibility to ensure that he or she is fed, clean and kept out of danger. A toddler cannot do these things for him or herself – they have to learn as they grow and develop to accept more and more responsibility for their own actions. This is a fairly clear-cut example, but there are many occasions when the distinction between what is your responsibility and what is not yours or is someone else's is not quite so black and white.

INTERNAL LOCUS OF CONTROL

There are some individuals who always internalize responsibility – whether it is theirs or not. This is a concept called 'internal locus of control'. They believe that most things in life are their responsibility, or their fault. They become anxious and worried over issues which they have no control over, but they *believe* must be their responsibility. These people feel that everyone should be happy, get along with others all the time, and it is their responsibility to ensure that this happens. If people are not having a good time it is their fault, and they quite often go to extreme measures to try and bring about peace and harmony.

The reality is that we are not responsible for other people's happiness, although we would want to be pleasant and kind to people and hope they respond accordingly. However, if they don't respond to us it is their choice not to. In the same way we cannot always be the peacemaker, or mediate between other people's differences. It is not our responsibility unless we are approached to become actively involved.

However, the good news with people who have a tendency to internalize responsibility is that they can be helped to get things into perspective and understand just what is within their sphere of influence, and what is not.

EXTERNAL LOCUS OF CONTROL

The reverse side of the coin concerns those who do not take any responsibility for their actions, and blame everyone else whilst denying their part in things. This is called 'external locus of control', and individuals with this kind of attitude can be very difficult to work with.

In a wider context this attitude often prevails when people find themselves in trouble with the police. For example:

- Shoplifting – 'The shopkeepers are asking for it, they shouldn't leave things where you can take them.'
- Traffic offences – 'It's stupid putting double yellow lines there, it's not my fault if there is nowhere else to park to get to the shops.'
- Stealing – 'If the state gave me more benefits I wouldn't have to steal anything to make ends meet.'
- Anti-social behaviour – 'It's not my fault I come from a broken home – what do you expect?'

… and so on.

Getting individuals to accept responsibility is not an easy task, especially when this type of belief is long standing and ingrained. However, it can be possible by challenging belief systems and asking the individual to supply 'evidence' which supports that thinking. Tool 17 will help you to do this.

Happily, most of us don't fall into these two extremes. Most of the time we are able to accept when something is our responsibility and when it is not. We are also pretty good at deciding when there is a certain amount of chance in a situation, whether that is good or bad luck, and realize that we cannot control all the variables all of the time.

METHOD

This tool can be used by individuals working on their own or by a manager with a member of staff. The tool consists of four scenarios, A, B, C and D, which are designed to assess whether individuals have an internal locus of control or an external one. Do they take responsibility for their actions, or do they tend to blame someone else? Each scenario has seven responses (a to g). Ask individuals to complete the questionnaire, ticking which responses they think apply to them. They can tick more than one. When they have completed the four scenarios, distribute the scoring sheet. Ask people to work out their overall scores for internal and external locus of control. Tell them to add up how many times they ticked 'g' and put the total in the box.

Locus of Control – Scenario A

Please tick those responses that apply to you.

You have just received the results of an important exam that you took a while ago. Unfortunately you have failed the exam. How would you react?

a) I would say that I should have revised harder. ☐

b) I would say that I was unlucky, that the wrong questions came up. ☐

c) I must have revised the wrong topics. ☐

d) My tutor wasn't very good, he should have told us what to expect. ☐

e) I didn't plan my time well in the exam. ☐

f) They didn't give us enough time to answer the questions. ☐

g) I can always try again another time. ☐

Locus of Control – Scenario B

Please tick those responses that apply to you.

You have a minor accident whilst driving your car. You were at a junction ready to pull out, started to do so then realized there was a car coming and you braked. The car behind runs into the back of you. What do you think and feel?

a) I should have kept going, then he wouldn't have hit me. ☐

b) The idiot was too close, he should have kept his distance. ☐

c) I was the one who hesitated, it's not fair to expect the other driver to know what I'm thinking. ☐

d) He should have known that there wasn't enough time for me to accelerate in front of the other car. ☐

e) I'm a lousy driver anyway. ☐

f) There are some bad drivers about, none of this was my fault. ☐

g) It happens, no point in getting worked up about it. ☐

Locus of Control – Scenario C

Please tick those responses that apply to you.

You take an urgent call from an important client. She wants you to find out some information. You agree to do that right away and phone her back. Then you get side-tracked and forget about it. She calls back and is furious. How do you feel?

a) I should have dealt with it and phoned her back. ☐

b) How am I expected to do a million things at once? ☐

c) I shouldn't have allowed myself to get caught up in something else. ☐

d) It's Jim's fault for asking me to get that file out for him. If he hadn't, I'd have remembered. ☐

e) It's my responsibility to deal with client's problems promptly and to deliver what I say I will. ☐

f) Clients have no understanding of what it's like to work here. ☐

g) You can only do your best, mistakes happen. ☐

Locus of Control – Scenario D

Please tick those responses that apply to you.

You enter a competition in a magazine. You are informed that you've won first prize. Apparently it was down to the tie-breaker you wrote. How would you react?

a) I'm really pleased with myself. ☐

b) That was lucky. ☐

c) I must have written a really good slogan. ☐

d) The odds on me winning this must be thousands to one. ☐

e) I knew I had it in me to win that competition. ☐

f) Everyone else's entry must have been poor. ☐

g) You win some, you lose some. ☐

REPRODUCED FROM *BULLYING IN THE WORKPLACE*, ELAINE DOUGLAS, GOWER, ALDERSHOT

Responses   **a**   **c**   and **e** relate to **internal locus of control**.

Responses   **b**   **d**   and **f** relate to **external locus of control**.

The final response (g) looks at how philosophical people are about life events, and the ability to put things into perspective. It is the attitude of 'c'est la vie' or 'these things happen' – there is little point worrying about it or getting upset.

Locus of Control Scoring Sheet

1. Score 1 for each response.
2. Add up the scores on internal and external locus of control to get an overall score.

	Internal		External	
Scenario A	a		b	
	c		d	
	e		f	
	Sub Total			
Scenario B	a		b	
	c		d	
	e		f	
	Sub Total			
Scenario C	a		b	
	c		d	
	e		f	
	Sub Total			
Scenario D	a		b	
	c		d	
	e		f	
	Sub Total			
	Overall Score			

Add up the number of responses to (g).   Total (g)

Look at the scores obtained from the score sheet:

Maximum internal locus of control = 12 (maximum).

Maximum external locus of control = 12 (maximum).

Getting it into perspective (g) = 4 (maximum).

INTERPRETING THE SCORES

You are looking for a balance between internal and external locus of control. In other words, an individual who can see that not everything is entirely their responsibility, or solely someone else's, that there are times when it is a combination of the two.

High scores on either dimension, without a counterbalance in the other, could indicate a strong tendency to take the blame or blame others.

For example:

Internal	External
8	3

This type of score suggests that the individual feels that most things in life are their responsibility. They do not take into account external circumstances or the part played by chance. On the other hand, the following scores:

Internal	External
3	8

indicate that this type of individual may well tend to abdicate responsibility and say that it is the fault of the other party or external circumstances.

An ideal profile would be one where the internal locus of control scores are moderate – between 5 and 8, and the external locus of control scores are low – between 1 and 4.

Preferred profile:

Internal	External
5–8	1–4

Low scores on either scale indicate some tendencies, but their preferences are not marked.

Responses to the (g) statements:

'I can always try again another time.'

'It happens, there's no point in getting worked up about it.'

'You can only do your best, mistakes happen.'

'You win some, you lose some.'

These responses indicate that the individual has the capability to take things in their stride and not get uptight about events. The degree to which they can do this will depend on the number of responses they give.

GIVING FEEDBACK – GUIDELINES FOR MANAGERS

It must be pointed out that this questionnaire is designed to highlight potential problems caused by the way in which individuals interpret events to be their responsibility or not. The scores show *tendencies* and *preferences* from a small sample and should not therefore be generalized to all situations.

When giving feedback to an individual from the results of this questionnaire, one must be careful to check out their interpretation of events. Phrases such as:

'Your responses to this scenario suggest …'

'If we look at scenario (A, B, C or D) can you explain why you ticked (a, d and f)?'

'What made you opt for …?'

… lead you into conversations in a non-threatening, non-judgemental way. Hopefully, the individual will then be able to expand on their reasons and motivations.

OUTCOMES

Once you as an individual (or as a manager) have an awareness of whether you or your member of staff tends to have an internal or external locus of control, you will be able to identify which tools in the toolkit are appropriate for you to work on. As mentioned earlier, Tool 17 in Chapter 8, which looks at belief systems, can be particularly useful. However, it is worth noting that if someone has a strong external locus of control score, they may be extremely resistant to change and believe that everyone else is out of step but them. If this is the case, you might want to discuss a referral to a more experienced professional.

TOOL 8: ANALYSE YOUR BEHAVIOUR QUESTIONNAIRE

PURPOSE

This questionnaire is designed to highlight certain behaviours which have been identified through research as being indicative of bullying behaviour. Some of the questions may not at first appear to have anything to do with intimidating behaviour, but they represent traits which have been found to be present in individuals who bully.

SITUATION

The questionnaire can be used as a development tool to enable managers to set goals with the individual. It can also be used as part of the appraisal process. Furthermore, if an individual has been accused of bullying, or there is a suspicion that he or she is not behaving appropriately, the questionnaire can be used in a one-to-one discussion with a manager or counsellor.

DESCRIPTION

The questionnaire has a series of statements which the individual has to respond to. They are asked to decide whether the statements apply to them 'Usually, Sometimes or Rarely'. These statements are followed by five further statements, to which the individual replies 'yes' or 'no'. Such statements relate to environmental factors which could put further strain on the individual. From this analysis it will be possible to see whether or not the individual is at risk of becoming or being a bully.

METHOD

Individuals can answer the questionnaire privately and score it themselves. If you are a manager asking someone to complete it, you will need to impress on them that they must answer the questions honestly – not how they think you would like them answered, or how they think they ought to answer.

If there are discrepancies between their analysis and, say, what you know of them, then it could be useful to ask someone else to fill it in on their behalf. For example, a work colleague who knows them well or their supervisor. Ask them to answer the questions with the individual in mind. What is their perception of the individual? They may not be able to answer all the questions, but probably enough to give you something against which to compare the original responses.

A word of caution in doing this! We are dealing with a highly emotive issue here. If you suspect that someone is a bully, and they complete the questionnaire and come up with a score that suggests there isn't a problem, you will have to tackle this sensitively. If you ask someone else to analyse the individual's behaviour, they (the suspected bully) may well feel threatened by this, or even that you disbelieve them.

You can get over this in a number of ways:

1 You can state from the outset that this is what you are going to do. You could say something along the lines of:

> 'I want you to fill this in for me. Think about how you see your behaviour and select the response which you believe is most appropriate to you. It's always interesting to see how others view us, so I'm going to ask --- to fill one in on your behalf. He/she knows you quite well, and we'll be able to compare them.'

2 You might want to do this as an exercise with all your staff so that you are not seen to be singling out a particular individual.
3 You could ask the individual to nominate someone to fill it out on their behalf. However, be careful – they might select someone whose behaviour is as bad as theirs.

Analyse Your Behaviour Questionnaire

Page 1 of 3

The following questionnaire is designed to get you to look at your behaviour in an honest and analytical manner. All of the questions are based on research which indicates that if you are prone to behaving in a certain way, your behaviour could be construed by others as intimidating or aggressive.

You might want to complete this questionnaire with your superior or line manager in mind. It may be that you don't have a problem, but perhaps they do!

Please tick (✓) which response is most like you.

A = Usually   **B** = Sometimes   **C** = Rarely

	A	B	C
1. I like to work in the 'here and now', I prefer not to think too far ahead.	☐	☐	☐
2. I consider that I am a forward thinker.	☐	☐	☐
3. I find it hard to deal with failure, especially in a personal sense.	☐	☐	☐
4. I do not have a good memory, and tend to forget things easily.	☐	☐	☐
5. I can be very selective in what I remember, and tend to filter out things which I find unpleasant or difficult to deal with.	☐	☐	☐
6. I can be economical with the truth at times.	☐	☐	☐
7. I believe that you have to look after number one in this life.	☐	☐	☐
8. When I make a decision I stick with it, I do not reverse or overturn my decisions.	☐	☐	☐
9. I consider myself to be a good listener.	☐	☐	☐
10. I feel that people should be able to take a joke, there are too many people who are over-sensitive.	☐	☐	☐
11. I demand high standards from others. I don't believe that people work hard enough.	☐	☐	☐

	A	B	C
12. I try and praise people, rather than pull them up for their shortcomings.	☐	☐	☐
13. I believe that others have more strengths and talents than myself.	☐	☐	☐
14. I believe that I can fulfil my dreams and become as successful as others.	☐	☐	☐
15. I think that my job is much harder than other people's, they have an easier time of it than me.	☐	☐	☐
16. I like to thank people for the work they do.	☐	☐	☐
17. I would not dream of taking someone else's work and passing it off as my own.	☐	☐	☐
18. It is acceptable to 'shift the goalposts' without consulting staff.	☐	☐	☐
19. I use sarcasm and/or criticism to get people to do what I want.	☐	☐	☐
20. My relationships with work colleagues tend to be rather superficial. It is unnecessary to develop a close rapport with them.	☐	☐	☐
21. I behave in the same way with my boss, my peers and my juniors.	☐	☐	☐
22. I suffer from mood swings, usually on a daily basis.	☐	☐	☐
23. I delegate well to my junior staff. I am happy to give them responsibility.	☐	☐	☐
24. I like to keep an eye on people to make sure that they are doing things to my satisfaction.	☐	☐	☐
25. I believe that the way I do thing is always the right way.	☐	☐	☐
26. I believe that if you apologize to someone it can be seen as a sign of weakness.	☐	☐	☐

REPRODUCED FROM *BULLYING IN THE WORKPLACE*, ELAINE DOUGLAS, GOWER, ALDERSHOT

Page 3 of 3

	A	B	C

27. I consciously try and use positive language and statements when talking over work issues with colleagues.

28. I try to treat all my staff fairly, I do not have favourites.

29. I suffer from indecisiveness.

30. I am always happy to take on extra responsibility. I see it as a challenge.

Please answer by ticking (✓) **Yes** or **No** to the following.

a) I have recently been promoted, and to be honest feel out of my depth. — Yes / No

b) I am worried that there are rumours going around that the company is contemplating redundancies. — Yes / No

c) I feel that I am under a great deal of pressure at work, and feel stressed by it. — Yes / No

d) My organization is employing more and more people on short-term contracts, rather than giving them permanent jobs. I am concerned for my future. — Yes / No

e) I have to work long hours and lots of overtime, not always through choice. — Yes / No

Scoring the Analyse Your Behaviour Questionnaire

Page 1 of 2

On the following questions:

1, 3, 4, 5, 6, 7, 10, 11, 13, 15, 17, 18, 19, 20, 22, 24, 25, 26 and 29

Score
  2 points for **Usually**
  1 point for **Sometimes**
  0 points for **Rarely**

On the following questions:

2, 8, 9,12,14,16, 21, 23, 27, 28 and 30

Score
  2 points for **Usually**
  1 point for **Sometimes**
  0 points for **Rarely**

Score Totals

  High   41–60

  Medium 21–40

  Low   0–20

Interpreting the scores

- **0–20** If your score falls within the 'Low' zone, then it is unlikely that your behaviour is bullying or intimidating. There may be some instances when you are under pressure that you may not behave as well as you would like, but it won't be a regular occurrence.

- **21–40** If your score falls within the 'Medium' zone, then you need to be much more aware of your behaviour. This is a warning light which suggests that you have a tendency to use bullying tactics to get others to do what you want or to ensure that things go your way. You are not a lost cause, however! Perhaps you are not aware of how what you say and do impacts on others. If this is the case, then you need to look at your behaviour more closely and start taking responsibility for your actions.

- **41–60** If you scored more than 41 you could be in real trouble. Scores within the 'High' zone suggest that you may well be insensitive to the needs of others and intolerant of their views. You really need to think hard about changing your behaviour. You may disagree with these statements and believe that what you practice is 'strong management', or that the confrontations you have with others can be put down to personality clashes. This is unlikely to be the case, but admitting that you are a bully is not easy. You are the only one who can change your behaviour, but you must first recognize it for what it is and accept that it needs to be changed. If you don't, you run the risk of going through life thinking that it's everyone else's fault but your own.

Supplementary Yes/No questions

If you answered 'Yes' to two or more of these supplementary questions, you could be more at risk than you think. Even if your score is within the 'Low' zone, the stress that can be caused by these environmental factors may make you more vulnerable and more likely to behave in a bullying manner.

OUTCOMES

You can use the results of the questionnaire to examine your behaviour and look at Chapter 8 to choose the right strategies to help you.

As a manager you might want to use the result as a discussion tool. For example, if it transpires that the individual is not a good listener you could look at this more closely. Find out why this is the case, for example are they always too busy or rushed? Find out if this happens across the board or are they selective, for example they don't listen to junior staff but have all the time in the world for the MD. Work out a strategy together, for example make time informally over coffee, or arrange a set time weekly. Use the tool on Active Listening (see Tool 15 in Chapter 8) to improve your skills.

You can examine individual statements and look at ways in which the individual can work at tackling their behaviour. For example:

> 'I like to keep an eye on people to make sure they are doing things to my satisfaction.'

This statement throws up issues of delegation and you may well be able to organize some training or coaching to improve their skills.

TOOL 9: ORGANIZATIONAL BULLYING QUESTIONNAIRE

PURPOSE

This questionnaire is designed to help you to discover whether your organization is supporting a bullying culture.

SITUATION

The questionnaire can be used as a culture survey, either by itself or in conjunction with the staff survey (see Tool 10 later in this chapter). As a manager you can use it to gather evidence that there is a problem when you are looking to put together an anti-bullying policy. If there is resistance from the top, then this would add weight to your argument. However, do not use this questionnaire if you are not prepared to follow it through with action. You will raise expectations that something will be done, and if nothing happens your workforce will be de-motivated.

There are 25 statements that are based on research into behaviours in an organization which are viewed as negative, unproductive or intimidating.

Individuals are asked to assess the statements and judge whether they apply to the organization 'Usually, Sometimes or Rarely'. Senior members of staff will be able to respond to all the questions, but junior members of staff may not be able to answer the following:

> 'When our organization needs to make staff cutbacks it saves money by manoeuvring people into leaving, rather than having to pay redundancy packages.'

> 'There is a strong tendency to work in the "here and now". Short-term thinking is evident at the expense of the long-term view.'

However, they should be able to make comments on the other statements.

It is probably better to distribute the questionnaire anonymously, collect the scripts and score them together. This can be done through the HR or personnel departments, or by an appointed person in a smaller organization.

METHOD

Distribute the questionnaire with a short explanation as to why you are doing this. Ask people to respond frankly and honestly and tell them that their scripts are confidential. To maintain confidentiality it is a good idea to send out envelopes with the questionnaires which are pre-addressed to an appropriate person or department. (This will be the person doing the scoring and possibly, but not necessarily, the person who will analyse the results.) People will then feel confident that answers cannot be traced back to them.

Organizational Bullying Questionnaire

Page 1 of 3

This questionnaire looks at some of the factors which have been identified through research as being indicators of a bullying organization.

A culture, which either actively promotes or passively condones aggressive behaviour from its employees, will not lead to an effective and efficient organization.

Look at the following statements and judge which apply to your organization. Be careful to look at the 'big picture', and not just how things are in your department. If the statements do just apply to your department, they could mean that there is a bullying sub-culture within your company, which may be as a result of a particular individual or group of individuals.

Please tick (✓) which response is most like your organization.

A = Usually   **B** = Sometimes   **C** = Rarely

	A	B	C
1. There is an obvious 'them and us' culture in the organization which is evidenced by senior management perks (e.g. higher than average pay rises, corporate hospitality events, frivolous expenditure on branded gifts).	☐	☐	☐
2. People skills are valued just as highly as budgetary and accounting skills.	☐	☐	☐
3. Lip service is paid to the corporate statement that 'people are our greatest asset'. This is not supported by the behaviour of managers.	☐	☐	☐
4. People who are recruited and promoted tend to be clones of senior management.	☐	☐	☐
5. Initiative, creativity and diversity are not acknowledged or rewarded in the company. I believe that these qualities are perceived as being threatening to senior staff.	☐	☐	☐
6. The company is one that challenges the status quo, and is always looking for new ways of doing things. People take calculated risks for the benefit of the company.	☐	☐	☐
7. In this organization managers adopt a consultative approach. There is a great emphasis placed on empowering the workforce.	☐	☐	☐

	A	B	C

8. Managers are not in touch with the reality of what goes on in the organization. They stick to plans and objectives when it is obvious to everyone else that they are inappropriate.

9. This is a very supportive organization, where people trust each other and work co-operatively.

10. When the organization needs to make staff cutbacks it saves money by manoeuvring people into leaving, rather than having to pay redundancy packages.

11. People these days are doing the same amount of work (or more) in fewer hours and for less money.

12. People are coerced into not taking holidays or to coming back to work when they should still be off sick.

13. Job security is threatened by managers insisting that we work compulsory overtime or unsociable hours. Refusal to comply means that those individuals are overlooked for promotion or labelled trouble makers.

14. There are plenty of opportunities for career advancement and development.

15. Money is spent on building up the image of the company, but it is difficult to get monies or resources for important and needy situations and circumstances.

16. This is a stable workforce, there is very little turnover of staff.

17. It is noticeable that the number of people taking sick leave has increased recently. Quite a number seem to be off with stress-related problems.

18. There is a pervasive atmosphere of negativity. Suspicion, hypersensitivity and hypervigilance are the norm.

19. The organization provides excellent customer service. This applies to both internal and external customers.

Page 3 of 3

	A	B	C

20. There is a strong tendency to work in the 'here and now'. Short-term thinking is evident at the expense of the long-term view. ☐ ☐ ☐

21. Morale is very high. For the most part people look forward to coming to work and enjoy what they do. ☐ ☐ ☐

22. There is a current trend to move people from full-time permanent contracts on to short-term ones. ☐ ☐ ☐

23. If there is a problem at work, there are people who are willing to listen and help. ☐ ☐ ☐

24. The organization follows a very rigid hierarchy. It is difficult for junior staff to access those higher up the ladder. ☐ ☐ ☐

25. There is an unwillingness to accept (or even outright denial) that bullying takes place. If you want to get on here you just keep your head down and don't make waves. ☐ ☐ ☐

Scoring Your Organizational Bullying Questionnaire

Page 1 of 1

On the following questions:

1, 3, 4, 5, 8, 10, 11, 12, 13, 15, 17, 18, 20, 22 and 25

Score
2 points for **Usually**
1 point for **Sometimes**
0 points for **Rarely**

On the following questions:

2, 6, 7, 9, 14, 16, 19, 21 and 23

Score
0 points for **Usually**
1 point for **Sometimes**
2 points for **Rarely**

Score Totals

High	31–50
Medium	16–30
Low	0–15

Interpreting the scores

- **0–15** If your score was in the 'Low' zone it is probably the case that your organization does not have a bullying culture. However, there may be some practices or attitudes which could be improved upon. It is better not to rest on your laurels and think that everything is fine – there is always room for improvement.

- **16–30** In the 'Medium' zone alarm bells should be ringing. Although these scores are in the medium range, there could be certain behaviours and approaches which give cause for concern. If you responded 'sometimes' to most of the statements it could mean that your organization is heading for trouble. If the relevant issues are not addressed it could mean that, within a short period of time, you could move into the 'High' zone.

- **31–50** This is the 'High' zone, and if your score falls within this range there is definitely a problem. There is strong evidence that a bullying culture pervades within the organization. It is likely that productivity and efficiency are compromised and that the workforce is demoralized and de-motivated. Maybe people will stay because they don't have any other alternatives, but many will be actively looking to leave or may already have done so. It is imperative that changes are made, and swiftly. The situation can be turned round, but only with the commitment and dedication of the decision makers.

OUTCOMES

As the manager who has initiated this, you will have to make a decision, possibly with the guidance from senior staff, as to what you do with the information. As stated earlier, you can use the findings to support your argument for introducing an anti-bullying policy and to convince sceptics that something needs to be done. However, you need to give some feedback to the employees who have completed the questionnaire. If you don't do this then you risk alienating and de-motivating your staff.

Having said this, they do not need to know all the facts and figures. Something along the lines of:

> 'The results of our questionnaire suggest that 75% of those who replied believe that our company is supporting a bullying culture. The survey (see Tool 10) also suggests that sadly a number of people have either experienced or witnessed bullying. As a company we are totally committed to ensuring that our staff are treated with dignity and respect. We intend to tackle this problem. Bullying and intimidating behaviour will not be tolerated. Our first steps will be to implement an anti-bullying policy in the company. This will be followed by training and a series of initiatives to ensure that we eradicate this behaviour. We will need your support in this, and look forward to working with you to ensure that our company builds and develops a positive and supportive environment for its employees.'

This kind of message can be e-mailed to everyone in the company. Posters, memos and communications can also be distributed so that all staff are aware of what is going to happen.

You can use Tool 10 (Staff Survey on Bullying) alongside this questionnaire. This will give you more specific information as to whether your employees have actually experienced bullying first hand. However, you need to be aware that the results of this survey may not necessarily tell the whole story, or indeed give an accurate picture. People's definitions of bullying can vary, and they may not be aware that the way they are being treated constitutes bullying. So even if the results of the questionnaire and survey suggest that bullying isn't too much of a problem, it is still a good idea to go ahead with the policy and training.

TOOL 10: STAFF SURVEY ON BULLYING

PURPOSE

This is a straightforward survey which can be used to gauge the extent of bullying in the organization.

SITUATION

As with Tool 9 (Organizational Bullying Questionnaire) this survey is designed to look at bullying in a 'corporate' sense – in other words a wider viewpoint. It can be used prior to the introduction of an anti-bullying policy and as a yardstick in the future to see whether the situation is better, the same or worse.

DESCRIPTION

There are two parts to the survey. The first gives demographic information (for example gender, age, race) which will help to identify whether there are any issues of harassment to do with these areas. However, if respondents feel that by answering these questions it would compromise their anonymity, they can leave this section out.

The second section is designed to find out the extent of the problem. It looks at whether people have been bullied directly and/or have witnessed bullying. It also asks respondents to 'tick' which behaviours (if any) they have experienced, by whom and for how long. Finally, if they have experienced bullying it asks whether they have been able to deal with the problem (either alone or with support), and if they haven't why this was the case.

It is quite a short survey, and can be completed in about ten minutes.

METHOD

As already mentioned, bullying is an extremely emotive issue and, therefore, any investigations you make must be done with care and sensitivity. As with Tools 6–9, people will be concerned about issues of confidentiality and will probably be offended if, for example, the survey is only distributed to a sample or certain individuals.

The best way to use the survey is to distribute it to all members of staff, having prepared them beforehand in a team meeting or briefing session. There is an explanatory introduction with the survey, but it is better to talk to people as well, so that you can answer any concerns or clear up any potential misunderstandings.

If you put the survey into an envelope it can be returned to the person collating the information and confidentiality is maintained.

Results can be collated in a number of ways, for example percentages, bar charts, pie charts or in a narrative form. The information you have gathered can be represented in a quantitative or qualitative way:

1 Quantitative
    - 75% of respondents have been bullied or witnessed bullying
    - 80% of bullying is over a period of time
    - 70% comes from managers/supervisors
    - 15% comes from colleagues
    - 12% comes from clients
    - 3% comes from junior members of staff.
2 Qualitative
    - People who have been bullied tend to keep the problem to themselves.
    - Most people who have experienced bullying feel ashamed and embarrassed and feel that if they reported it they wouldn't be believed.

Whichever way you choose, and it could be a combination of the two, the results need to be clear and unambiguous.

Staff Survey on Bullying

Page 1 of 5

This survey will be treated in the strictest confidence, and we do not want you to identify yourself or to name anyone who you think is behaving as a bully. It is an information gathering exercise.

Purpose of Survey

We are trying to find out whether bullying is a problem in this organization. If it is, we need to discover the extent of the problem and take steps to eradicate it.

We are also trying to determine whether there are any issues around sexual harassment and discrimination on the grounds of race, disability or age. However, we understand that some people may not feel comfortable disclosing this information and you may prefer not to answer these specific questions. This is fine. You are under no obligation. We would ask that if you can, you tell us about your experiences. The more we know, the better chance we have of sorting out any problems.

Thank you for your co-operation.

Part 1

If you feel that these questions would compromise your anonymity, please leave them out.

Please circle.

Gender: Male   Female

Age: 16–25   26–35   36–45   over 45

Race: White   African   Afro Caribbean   Asian   Oriental   Other

Country of origin: Great Britain   Other

Disability: Yes   No

Part 2

If bullying is a problem in this organization, the responses from these questions will help us to understand the extent of it.

1. Have you experienced bullying and/or harassment at work? (please tick)

    Yes ☐   No ☐

2. Was it a 'one off' or more than one incident? (please tick)

    One off ☐   More than one ☐

3. Have you witnessed other people being bullied? (please tick)

    Yes ☐   No ☐

4. Have you been subjected to any of the following behaviours and found them to be offensive, unwanted or intimidating? (please tick all which apply)

innuendo ☐	staring ☐	gestures ☐
being 'sent to Coventry' ☐	displays of lewd or pornographic material ☐	physical abuse or intimidation ☐
threat of job security ☐	unreasonable work demands ☐	sarcasm or putdowns ☐
unfair criticism of your work ☐	denial of leave and/or promotion opportunities ☐	your ideas or work being passed off as someone else's ☐

Page 4 of 5

5. Who exhibited this behaviour? (If you have been bullied by more than one person, please tick all those which apply.)

   A manager/supervisor ☐   A colleague ☐

   A junior member of your staff ☐   A client ☐

6. Have you ever tried to do anything about being bullied? (please tick)

   Yes ☐   No ☐

7. If 'Yes' did you (please tick all those which apply)

   Tell someone at work? ☐   If so, who?   Friend ☐

   Colleague ☐

   Manager/supervisor ☐

   Personnel/HR ☐

   Tell someone at home? ☐

   Tell the police? ☐

   Tell a lawyer? ☐

   Speak to a counsellor? ☐

Was the problem sorted out?

Totally ☐   Partly ☐   Not at all ☐

8. If you didn't try to do anything about the bullying, why was this? (please tick all of those which apply)

Felt ashamed and embarrassed ☐   Worried about reprisals ☐

Felt 'I wouldn't be believed' ☐   Felt guilty, that it was 'my fault' ☐

See it as 'normal' behaviour ☐   Felt it wouldn't make any difference ☐

Felt 'I was making mountains out of molehills' ☐

Other (please specify) _____

9. Did you try and tackle the person directly?   Yes ☐   No ☐

10. If 'Yes' did the bullying stop?   Yes ☐   No ☐

Thank you for completing this questionnaire.

OUTCOMES

Having carried out the survey you need to do something with the findings. People who have taken the time to complete it are entitled to know what the results are. You might decide to distribute the findings in their entirety to the staff, or to issue a summary. However, this needs to be followed (for example, in a meeting) to inform staff about what will happen next. A survey in itself is only one of the first stages of dealing with the problem. Depending on the results of the survey and your current situation, you may want to consider the following:

- setting up an anti-bullying policy (as described in Chapter 2)
- setting up training for awareness raising and/or specific training for specialized staff roles (as described in Chapters 3 and 4)
- examining existing systems to see whether they can be improved, for example appraisals, lines of communication, team issues.

If you feel that there is a lot of work to be done, you may need to appoint someone to project manage the implementation of a rolling programme. It would be their job to co-ordinate all the different elements of an anti-bullying programme and to ensure that it happens and the impetus is not lost.

Chapter 8
Dealing with behaviour

This chapter contains practical, 'hands on' tools which will help you to change your behaviour (or that of your staff), and also reframe the thinking which drives this behaviour. You will find the following tools:

- Tool 11: Scripting
- Tool 12: Rehearsal
- Tool 13: Broken Record
- Tool 14: Saying 'No'
- Tool 15: Active Listening
- Tool 16: Anger Reduction
- Tool 17: Challenging and Changing Thinking
- Tool 18: Confidence Boosters
- Tool 19: Harnessing Emotional Intelligence
- Tool 20: Making an Action Plan
- Tool 21: Relaxation Techniques
- Tool 22: Making a Buddy.

Each tool is described fully, with guidance as to when and how to use it. Some of these tools can be used in conjunction with others, and advice is given as to how to do this.

TOOL 11: SCRIPTING

PURPOSE

Scripting is a technique which, as the name implies, enables you to prepare in advance. It suits a variety of situations from large board meetings to a conversation with the office junior. It is based on win–win principles where each party feels that they have achieved something.

SITUATION

Use this technique when you need to prepare yourself for a situation. It could be that you need to think through a meeting that you have arranged with a colleague, your boss or a junior member of staff. It may be that situations seem to recur where you are asked to take on more work than you can handle or when you have to work with someone on a particular project whom you find 'spiky' and difficult.

DESCRIPTION

The good thing about Scripting is that you can work things out in advance, and once you have written your script you can rehearse it until you feel comfortable. You can also play out 'worst possible scenario' and 'best possible scenario', so that you are thoroughly prepared. If you are anticipating a problematic encounter with your boss, or 'that woman' from accounts then you can anticipate how they might react and how you would deal with this. Preparation is the key. The more you go over something, the less likely you are to be caught out by the unexpected.

Remember the saying:

'Forewarned is forearmed.'

METHOD

How to work out your script:

1 Identify the situation or set of circumstances you find problematic.
2 Think through what your needs are.
3 Work out a way in which you can acknowledge the other person's needs while putting forward your own.
4 Decide whether you are able to compromise to reach agreement, or whether you are unable to accommodate the other individual.
5 Decide on the outcome that you can live with.

The following scenarios outline the technique.

Scenario 1

You find it difficult to say no to your pushy team leader when they want you to work late. Invariably they don't give you much notice.

The script may go something like this:

- Acknowledging their needs:

    'I realize that this piece of work needs finishing.'

- Stating your own needs:

    'However, I have commitments this evening and you haven't given me enough time to make alternative arrangements.'

- The compromise might be:

    'I can stay an extra half an hour, but I'm afraid no longer than that.'

- The alternative might be:

    'I'm sorry I can't help you this time, but I can stay longer the day after tomorrow if that's any help.'

These alternatives put you back in control of the situation, but equally they indicate that you are not just being awkward for the sake of it. It is the responsibility of your team leader to prioritize work loads, and barring emergencies they should be managing the time of the team effectively.

Negotiated overtime is a different matter, as this indicates a joint problem solving approach.

If things get tricky, use the Broken Record (Tool 13) approach to maintain your case.

Scenario 2

One of your colleagues is always making wisecracks about the way you dress. You have told them to shut up on more than one occasion, but they say you can't take a joke.

The script may look something like this:

- Acknowledging their needs or views:

    'I realize you think it's funny to make remarks about my appearance ...'

- Stating your needs:

    '... but I don't find them funny and they upset me. I would like you to keep your thoughts to yourself.'

On this occasion there is no room for compromise, and indeed there are consequences should he or she persist:

    'If you carry on in this way I will have to speak to my manager about it.'

Of course there are other ways of dealing with this type of situation. For example, you may try laughing it off and pretending it doesn't upset you – they may grow tired of harassing you because it doesn't provoke a reaction.

However, if they can't (or won't) take a hint and using humour does not sort it out, you may need to prepare a script along the lines illustrated above.

Scenario 3

You are new to the company and are keen and enthusiastic. However, you soon realize that your arrival has given some people the opportunity to dump all the rotten jobs on you, despite them not being in your job description.

In this situation you can tackle it in one of two ways.

The first would be to speak to each individual in turn and ask them to explain why they have off-loaded on to you. The second would be to speak to your supervisor. This scenario looks at the latter.

The script may go something like this:

- Acknowledging their needs:

    'I understand that x, y and z have to be done as they are a necessary part in the running of the department.'

- Stating your own needs:

    'However, although I accept that I have to do my fair share, I am unhappy about being dumped on.'

- The compromise might be:

    'I will happily take on x and part of y, but I feel the rest should be shared out.'

OUTCOMES

Using a script will give you more confidence and more control over situations. When you have identified the situation that needs a script, and have worked out a suitable one, you need to practise it. This is where Rehearsal comes in (see Tool 12).

TOOL 12: REHEARSAL

PURPOSE

Rehearsal is a means of practising your Scripting technique (see Tool 11).

SITUATION

As with Scripting, it is used to help you to prepare for a situation which you find daunting and difficult.

DESCRIPTION

When you have your script there are two ways of rehearsing it. The first is to pretend you are talking to someone in an empty chair and the second is to work with someone you trust and feel at ease with.

METHOD

The empty chair

- Look at best outcome and worst outcome.
- Do not focus entirely on the negative outcome.
- Generate responses that the other individual may come up with.
- Work out ways of responding yourself.
- Challenge any negative thinking and change it to positive, for example:
  - from *'I'll never be able to do this'*
  - to *'I can do this.'*

With a partner

- Brief them as to the scenario you're working on.
- Get them to prepare their script – if necessary asking them to be as difficult as possible.
- Act out the scene.
- Stay calm if things appear to be getting heated.
- Remember your Broken Record technique (see Tool 13).
- Maintain eye contact.
- Try to smile.
- Practise slow breathing (see Tool 21 on Relaxation Techniques).

OUTCOMES

This may seem very awkward and stilted at first, and won't necessarily come naturally. Don't worry. The more you rehearse the easier it will become. As you practise try to work out what the other person is likely to say, and how they may react (for example, by paying attention to their body language). By doing this you will be thoroughly prepared.

Psychological research shows that the more we prepare for something, and anticipate possible outcomes, the better we will cope with the situation when it arises.

TOOL 13: BROKEN RECORD

PURPOSE

This is an excellent technique to use in conjunction with Scripting (Tool 11). Quite often people get stuck when it comes to keeping to the format of the script. They find it difficult to maintain their stance when it comes to stating their needs, especially in the face of opposition.

SITUATION

'Broken Record' is yet another tool in the repertoire towards becoming more assertive. It is probably best used in situations where you find yourself searching for the right words to respond towards someone who is being aggressive towards you. In these circumstances it is unlikely that your brain will generate a quick response, and you will probably find yourself tongue-tied. If this is the case, this technique will help you out.

DESCRIPTION

The 'Broken Record' technique does not lead to stimulating dialogue, but it can help to put the brakes on if you feel that you are not being listened to. In essence, what you do is to keep on repeating yourself.

METHOD

If we take the example of someone trying to coerce you into doing work for them, you could say:

> 'John, I need to finish this report before I type these letters for you.'

Whatever John says next you just repeat your statement.

It is difficult for the other person if they are being blocked in this way. Since it takes two to argue, this effectively stops any argument in its tracks.

Of course the other person will soon start to feel frustrated and could get more irritated. If you can stand your ground at this point you are almost there. The ball is in their court to come up with some suggestions as to how the situation can be resolved. However, if you feel confident you can propose some solutions which can then be discussed.

Throughout all of this you need to remain calm and controlled. You may not necessarily feel like this, but appearances can be deceptive. No one will see your heart beating nineteen to the dozen. Give the impression of being in control and people will assume you are. Practise relaxed breathing to help you (see Tool 21).

Examples

Here follow two scenarios to illustrate this technique.

A simple scenario could be:

> Mrs Brown: 'I bought this dress from you yesterday and I've just found that all the stitching is coming undone. I would like my money back please.'
>
> Shop assistant: 'I'm sorry we don't give refunds. You can have a credit note or choose something else.'
>
> Mrs Brown: 'I don't want a credit note or another garment. I would like my money back.'
>
> Shop assistant: 'It's the shop's policy not to give refunds.'
>
> Mrs Brown: 'Then you'd better let me speak to your manager. I want a refund.'

… and so on.

Here is a more detailed scenario:

Ben is a recently promoted supervisor in a small administration department. He has been promoted from within the department and one member of staff in particular is resentful of this. Tony believes he should have got the post and is making Ben's life a misery by producing sloppy work and not taking any notice of him – or coming up with lame excuses – when Ben asks him to get on with it.

> Ben: 'Tony could you please re-do this quarterly report. I'm afraid it's too thin and we need more information.'
>
> Tony: 'I'm not doing it again, I've got enough to do.'
>
> Ben: 'Tony, I need you to spend more time on it. It's not good enough in its present state.'
>
> Tony: 'I've told you I've other things to do – get someone else to do it.'
>
> Ben: 'I'm asking you. This report needs working on.'
>
> Tony: 'You're always pulling me up for my work – you've got it in for me.'
>
> Ben: 'Tony, I'm asking you to amend this report.'
>
> **N.B.** Notice Ben is not rising to the bait.
>
> Tony: 'How am I expected to finish all this lot off as well? Anyway, when's the meeting?'
>
> Ben: 'The meeting is next Friday and I want you to work on this report, and let me have it by Thursday at the latest.'
>
> Tony: 'I'll never get it done in time.'
>
> Ben: 'I will speak to you on Monday and see how far you have got.'

This is quite a sophisticated broken record as Ben manages to reiterate his request in a number of different ways. He does not stray from the point and he does not get drawn in to fighting off any of Tony's excuses.

OUTCOMES

If you combine the broken record technique with some of the relaxation techniques outlined in Tool 21 you will find that you successfully fend off any bullying behaviour. As you become more confident and in control of the situation, you can use other strategies, for example, Scripting (Tool 11) and Saying 'No' (Tool 14).

If you still feel daunted by the prospect of standing firm, you might want to look at Challenging and Changing Thinking (Tool 17). It may be that the underlying belief you have about yourself is that you are not really worthy of being treated well. If this is the case, use Confidence Boosters (Tool 18) to help you to reaffirm your value as a person.

TOOL 14: SAYING 'NO'

PURPOSE

Some people find it hard to say 'no'. This may be to their boss, partner, children or friends. They feel guilty and sometimes selfish if they refuse a request, or they might not want to cause offence. Unfortunately, not being able to say 'no', means that you get taken for granted and are more likely to be pushed around.

By accepting that your needs are as important as the next person's, you will start to increase your own feelings of self-worth and self-respect. This technique will show you that it is okay to say no, if you are asked to do something you don't want to do, or if the request is an unreasonable one.

SITUATION

This is a useful tool to use at work when, for example, your supervisor or manager is piling work on to you with unrealistic time frames, or expects you to take on a task that you haven't been trained to do or have insufficient knowledge of.

DESCRIPTION

Saying 'no' is about turning down or refusing a request. However, the skill is in how you say it! If your refusal comes in an aggressive form, then it will create more problems than it solves.

METHOD

When faced with a request, you need to be able to come up with a response which is neither passive (so that you give in) nor aggressive (so that you refuse, but bite someone's head off in the process).

Here are a couple of scenarios to illustrate the technique.

Scenario 1

Your work colleague has left things until the last minute and is now pushed for time to complete an important letter to a client and prepare some figures for the weekly team meeting to be held in the morning. They ask you to input the figures while they write the letter. They are always disorganized, and you have your own work to do for the meeting. If you do as they ask it will mean either working through your lunch or staying on after work. What do you say?

Passive answer:

> 'Well, all right then, I'll help you out but I'm a bit busy.'

This leads to feelings of conflict, resentment and lowered self-respect.

Aggressive answer:

> 'I haven't got time for that, you should get your act together and then you might not be doing things at the last minute.'

This leads to feelings of guilt and anger.

Assertive answer:

> 'Actually I'm up to my ears in it as well, so I don't think I can help. Why don't you have a word with Anne (line manager) and see if she can come up with any suggestions?'

This leads to feelings of increased confidence and elevated self-esteem.

Scenario 2

A work colleague needs time off to go to a family wedding. They are nervous about approaching their supervisor and want you to do it for them. This sort of thing has happened before and you are fed up with sorting out their problems. What do you say?

Passive answer:

> 'Oh go on then, if you want.'

This leads to feelings of resentment and irritation.

Aggressive answer:

> 'Do it yourself, I'm not your nursemaid.'

This leads to feelings of guilt and annoyance with the individual and self.

Assertive answer:

> 'I really think this is something you should do yourself, but if you're a bit nervous we can talk through what you could say.'

This leads to increased self-respect and feeling good about one's self.

OUTCOMES

Saying 'no' will help you to feel better about yourself. However, as the examples illustrate it needs tact and diplomacy so that you do not upset or offend people. If you still feel unhappy about doing this you may have an underlying belief that it is wrong to say 'no'. If this is the case you will find Tools 17 and 18 helpful as they focus on belief systems and improving confidence.

TOOL 15: ACTIVE LISTENING

PURPOSE

When you enter into a dialogue with someone it is essential that you listen to what they have to say. Too often people are preparing responses in their head because they are completely focused on their point of view and are not prepared to listen to what the other person thinks or feels.

It is also important that an individual should be seen to be listening. Quite often people do listen carefully, but they give the impression of being disinterested or preoccupied. Active listening is the cornerstone of any communication.

SITUATION

Active listening skills are invaluable in a number of situations, for example interviewing, meetings, coaching, mentoring and appraisals. Being aware of how to listen to someone will help in building relationships at work and in our personal lives.

DESCRIPTION

There is an expression, 'We hear, but we do not listen.' This is very true. How many times have you been guilty of saying 'Sorry, what did you say?'. Our mind may be elsewhere, we may be distracted or we may have tuned out or switched off, perhaps because we have heard it all before.

Active listening is about *showing* that you are listening by being attentive to the other person. This is done through what we say and how we present ourselves, in other words through verbal communication and non-verbal communication (sometimes referred to as body language).

METHOD

You can demonstrate active listening by:

- maintaining sensible eye contact – not evasive or staring
- making sure your body is angled towards the other person, but avoiding face to face as this can be interpreted as confrontational distance
- nodding head or saying 'umm' to keep the conversation going
- waiting for a natural break before replying – not interrupting
- checking understanding from time to time by summarizing and clarifying issues.

Be aware of:

- becoming distracted by what might be going on around you
- fiddling with papers, pens and so on and appearing distracted

- showing irritation through toe-tapping, sighing or making tutting noises.

Unfortunately there are things which prevent us from listening actively. Here are some examples:

- Glazed look – the expression that tells the other person we are not interested or our mind is elsewhere.
- Triggers – some words, phrases or concepts hook into our own prejudices and either cause us to stop listening or to get angry.
- On-off – we think a lot faster than we speak and our mind can race ahead or start planning what we want to say next.
- Switch off – if we disagree with the other person's point of view or our own beliefs are being challenged we can turn off.

Body language is non-verbal communication, and it is important because it can promote or discourage active listening. The way we sit or stand, our proximity to the person we are listening to, our gestures and tone of voice, are important. We can unwittingly negate what we are saying or how we are perceived by others through negative body language.

The following are do's and don'ts when considering body language.

Do's

- Position your body towards the other person (that is, crossed legs pointing towards them not away), and lean slightly forward.
- Incline your head to one side – it indicates interest.
- Keep your feet still – no shuffling.
- Keep your tone of voice even, try not to let it increase in volume or pitch.

Don'ts

- Don't fold your arms – keep 'open' posture.
- Don't stand too close, it invades personal space.
- Don't wave your arms or hands about too much.
- **Never** point with your finger to emphasize a point.

OUTCOMES

You will need to practise listening in an active way. As it becomes more automatic you will notice that people will talk to you more readily if they feel that you are interested in them. You don't necessarily have to agree with what they say, but if others believe that they are being listened to and taken seriously it will make all the difference.

TOOL 16: ANGER REDUCTION

Some people seem to have much shorter fuses than others. It doesn't take them long to 'lose it'. Quite often this is due to a combination of factors. It can be personality, how you were brought up (was yours a household where people regularly erupted over something and nothing – or did they brood and sulk)? Or, it could be certain events that trigger off a response. It may even be your interpretation of events which leads you to feel angry.

Quite often when we become angry about something we fuel it and keep it going. The conversations we have in our head (our internal dialogue) perpetuates the problem rather than lets go of it. We brood on what has happened or what has been said and this affects both our behaviour and our mood.

PURPOSE

Anger reduction techniques are based on changing or handling aggression – which is the observable behaviour of anger. Anger is an emotion, and sometimes it is important to get angry about issues – but we need to manage it constructively. When anger produces aggressive behaviour it needs to be controlled.

SITUATION

Anger reduction techniques are very useful for defusing difficult and tricky situations. For example, in a busy, pressured department it is often the case that everyone is on a short fuse with each other. When individuals are stressed and under pressure, they don't always observe social niceties! These techniques can be discussed and practised by groups as well as individuals. They could form part of a stress management programme or an analysis of group dynamics.

Similarly the techniques can be applied to specific individuals. As a manager you may be aware of certain individuals who seem to be having problems controlling their temper. If the problem is addressed through one-to-one discussion (done privately and unhurriedly), solutions can be discussed and different strategies tried out. It might be useful to incorporate this into an action plan which can be monitored and reviewed (see Tool 20).

DESCRIPTION

Anger reduction techniques are intended to help understand where anger comes from and how it can be managed and controlled more effectively. The techniques can be accessed by individuals working on their own or with line managers or colleagues.

METHOD

Before we can reduce anger, we need to understand where it comes from and what the triggers are. Consider the following:

1. We are prevented from doing something we want or need to do. For example, we cannot get on with our work because of constant interruptions.
2. We are promised something and it doesn't materialize. For example, we are told at an appraisal that we will be promoted and it doesn't happen.
3. We feel threatened – either physically or psychologically. This brings on the 'flight or fight' response associated with stress. For example, rumours suggest that some redundancies are imminent and so we target our anger and aggression towards those we feel are responsible.
4. We are attacked – this can be to do with a physical attack, but it may be attacks on our self-esteem or integrity. For example, we are constantly criticized and told we are useless. Some will come out fighting, others will withdraw.
5. Failure – this drives very strong emotions including anger. Sometimes we set ourselves impossible goals and become frustrated and angry when we don't reach them.

Added to the above is the way in which we interpret events. If we believe that others are working to some hidden agenda, or are doing things deliberately to 'get at' us, we will react more forcefully.

When you have identified what makes you angry, you will have a better understanding of how to handle difficult situations.

Examples

These are some suggestions that you can try out.

- **Walk away**: If you feel that you might lose control, it is better to withdraw and cool down. However, storming out of a room solves nothing. Let the other person know – in as civil a way as you can manage – that you are unable to continue this discussion.

- **Count to ten**: It seems a bit hackneyed, but it works. It helps you to formulate a more reasoned response and not speak before your brain is engaged.

- **Be aware**: What are your trigger points, what is likely to make you mad? If you know what winds you up, you have more of a chance of avoiding confrontational situations.

- **Consequences**: Before you get into a situation that is difficult to get out of, think through what the consequences of losing your temper (especially at work) may be. For example, you will develop a reputation, you might get passed over for promotion, and you will make life difficult for yourself. It is about accepting responsibility for your own actions.

- **Change your thinking**: Try to put a different interpretation on a situation. If someone walks past you without speaking don't assume that they are ignoring you and feel affronted. Maybe they are preoccupied or maybe they haven't got their glasses on! There is always an alternative perspective to things.

- **Practise slow breathing**: When we get angry our heart rate increases and we breathe quickly and shallowly. Take deep breaths in through the nose and out through the mouth to a count of ten. It will help you to calm down.
- **Take it out on something else**: Release your aggression safely. This might mean thumping a punchbag (if available!), going somewhere where you can let out a string of expletives without offending or upsetting anyone, or writing down your thoughts and feelings – for your eyes only.
- **Distract yourself**: If possible, go for a walk to take time out and think about something pleasant – a forthcoming holiday or night out. Resist the temptation to plot to get your own back.
- **Cultivate a sense of humour**: Instead of boiling up inside try and see the funny side of things. This isn't always easy, but if you can do it, it is a very effective way of keeping things in perspective.
- **Is it important?**: Is this issue really something that warrants raising your blood pressure? Will it be important in a month's or a week's time – or even tomorrow?
- **Practise assertiveness**: This is the middle ground between behaving aggressively and passively and is much more effective in achieving results (see Tools 11 and 12).
- **Empathize**: How is the other person going to feel if you rant and rave? Would you like to be on the receiving end of your tongue lashing?
- **Let go**: If you brood on an event – what has been said or done – then you keep your anger going. It is like putting coal on the fire. You need to let it go, get rid of it and dump it. The strategies listed above should help you to do this.

It is better not to attempt too much at once. Select a couple of things that you feel will work for you, and try them out for at least a month or two. It does take a while to 'throw off' old habits and behaviours.

OUTCOMES

Using these techniques will help you to feel calmer and more in control. By changing your own behaviour you will change the way in which others react and respond to you.

There are other tools in this section of the toolkit that may help you further. Have another look at the matrix at the beginning of the toolkit to identify which ones are particularly relevant to your situation.

TOOL 17: CHALLENGING AND CHANGING THINKING

BELIEF SYSTEMS

What we believe affects our attitude, which in turn affects our behaviour (see Figure 8.1).

If someone is behaving aggressively it is often the case that they have irrational beliefs or some kind of skewed outlook.

Changing people's beliefs is incredibly difficult. This is because they are usually deep rooted. However, it is not impossible. By challenging what they accept as a 'truism', by getting them to support their belief with hard evidence, people can have a shift of thinking.

Figure 8.1 Belief systems

BELIEFS ⇔ **ATTITUDE** ⇔ **BEHAVIOUR**

PURPOSE

The purpose of challenging belief systems is to try and encourage individuals to examine what they believe is true about themselves and others, and to look objectively at these beliefs to judge whether or not they are valid. If the values and beliefs are outmoded or irrational and skewed in some way, it becomes possible to look for alternatives which are more appropriate.

SITUATION

Helping people to examine their belief systems can be useful if they are showing either passive or aggressive tendencies. For example, if people are floundering because they can't stand up for themselves and consequently are taking on too much, their beliefs may be:

'It's wrong to say no.'

'You must do everything you can to help others, even if there's a cost to yourself.'

'I have to do everything that people in authority tell me to do.'

'I'm only a junior member of staff, so I expect to be treated like this.'

'They wouldn't give me this work if they didn't feel I could handle it.'

'You will look foolish if you admit you don't know what to do.'

'Everyone else is more important/significant than me.'

If someone is behaving in an aggressive or bullying manner their beliefs might be:

'I'm superior to the next person because I've had a better education, have more money etc. therefore, their opinions don't matter.'

> 'In this world it's every man for himself, you've got to get in there first.'

> 'It's a sign of weakness to admit that you can't do something, so it's better to cover up or deflect the blame onto someone else.'

If someone is qualified by experience and has few formal qualifications their beliefs might be:

> 'You don't need degrees to get on in this world, those that have think they know it all.'

Other beliefs which can lead to unacceptable behaviour might be:

> 'You can't trust anyone in authority (for example, managers, union officials). There will always be a "them and us" culture, it's inevitable.'

> 'Black people are inherently lazy, that's why you've got to keep on top of them.'

> 'Women don't think as logically as men, you can't take them seriously.'

… and so on. It becomes apparent how these beliefs drive attitudes and behaviour.

If your organization has a problem with racial or sexual harassment and/or bullying, then you might find that the beliefs illustrated here are prevalent.

DESCRIPTION

As a 'tool' this is rather different from some of the other techniques discussed because you cannot say to someone 'go away and try this'. It is more an approach to facilitate discussion about why people behave as they do, and offers a structure to probe and explore what drives people to do what they do.

METHOD

There are two ways in which this particular tool can be used:

1 In a one-to-one conversation between an employee and his or her manager.
2 As a self-help tool for individuals to develop self-awareness.

In the first instance a manager would:

- identify the situations and/or people that seem to be creating problems for the individual in question
- draw up a working hypothesis as to what might be happening
- test their hypothesis with the individual
- based on the feedback they get, then, if appropriate, challenge the belief system by providing evidence or facts which do not support it
- encourage the individual to consider a different interpretation of the situation and/or to suggest ways in which things could be viewed differently.

As an individual it is extremely difficult to challenge your own belief systems. These are part of your unique persona, and it would be virtually impossible for you to do this on your own. The most effective way to examine your beliefs, attitude and behaviour (assuming that you are able to admit that you have a problem) is to work with someone whom you trust and whose views you respect. Try this formula:

- Identify the situations and/or people that seem to be creating problems for you.
- Pinpoint specifically what it is that you do in these situations, that is, what you say, how you say it and how you behave.
- Check out with a friend who knows you well if you are being honest with yourself. Is your interpretation accurate or are you minimizing what happens? This is tricky! If you have asked someone to help, you must be prepared to listen to them, even if it is something you don't want to hear.
- Try and work out with your friend what it is that drives this behaviour. Is it a recent thing, or have you always behaved in this way? Do you react like this in every situation, or is it situation specific? Does it happen all the time, or only when you are stressed? (It may help at this point to read through the models of behaviour in Chapter 6. These will give you insight into your behaviour.)
- Look at the beliefs outlined earlier. Do any of them apply to you? Does your behaviour stem from lack of belief in yourself, low confidence or poor self-esteem?
- Check out with your friend if the beliefs you have about yourself and others hold credence. Look for evidence to challenge them, and try and work out how you might be able to put a different interpretation on things.

It must be emphasized that this work is not easy. It will take time for people to rethink their values and beliefs (if indeed they are able to at all). However, it is worthwhile. You can provide all kinds of techniques, for example assertiveness tools, anger reduction and so on, but if people don't actually believe that they can change, they will not 'buy into' it. Helping people to reach this level of self-awareness requires patience and skill, but in a sense it is fundamental to changing behaviour.

Example

The following case study illustrates how a manager might be able to work with an employee on challenging beliefs.

John is in his late 40s and has worked for his company for over 20 years. The company sells life assurance and pensions, and John is a good reliable worker with a solid and steady reputation. He always meets targets although doesn't often exceed them. He is well regarded by his employers, but is perceived by many as being a bit pedantic and staid.

The company has gone through a period of rapid expansion and over the last 12 months the sales force has expanded. Of these newcomers there are three, Dan, Penny and Colin, who are in their early 20s – fresh out of college and full of enthusiasm, and a fourth, Pam, who has returned to work having had her family and who is a similar age to John.

Mike, who is John's sales manager, has noticed that John seems to be making life difficult for the three youngsters, but gets on fine with Pam. John is sarcastic with Colin when he talks about his sales figures. He is bad-tempered with Penny when she asks for help or advice, and appears to instigate confrontations with Dan over very trivial matters. Mike decides that he must tackle the problem with John.

This is what happened when Mike used the framework given earlier:

- Identification of situations and/or people that are creating problems.

    Mike felt that there was a real problem in the way that John behaved towards Dan, Penny and Colin. He felt that John was behaving in an intimidating way and deliberately engineering and creating problems. This didn't happen with every member of staff, John was selective, and it had only recently become evident.

- Working hypothesis

    Mike felt that perhaps John felt threatened by the three younger sales people, or maybe he was jealous of them in some way. He thought that possibly John was opposed to those with a college education (particularly as he didn't have one), and resented the success that Dan, Penny and Colin were having.

- Testing hypothesis

    Mike discussed his thoughts with John. First of all he outlined the problems as he saw them. John initially was very defensive. He felt that it was not his fault and that the others were to blame. However, as Mike had witnessed a scene the previous day which was orchestrated by John, he had to admit albeit reluctantly that maybe he had been a bit difficult.

    Mike put forward reasons why he felt that there were problems:
    – Did John believe that in some way his position was in jeopardy?
    – Did John feel that they were getting all the breaks or having an easier time of it?
    – Was he dismissive of their qualifications?

- Using feedback

    John denied that he felt threatened by their success or that he was jealous (although Mike wasn't entirely convinced). He launched into a tirade about 'bloody graduates, think they know it all, you can't beat experience' and so on. Mike realized that part of John's problem was his inherent belief that years of experience doing a job were far superior to what a rookie straight from college could do. He felt that John was angry and resentful towards them and was displaying this in bad temper and bullying tactics.

However, Mike also realized that to point out that Dan, Penny and Colin were each pulling in twice as much business as John, would inflame the situation, even though there was hard evidence that John's beliefs were flawed. He decided to take a slightly different tack, by pointing out that there was merit in both experience and qualifications. It was not necessarily a case of one being 'better' than the other – both had value. After much debate John became less aggressive and said that he was prepared to consider what Mike was saying.

Mike also made a note that John would undoubtedly benefit from some in-house training in self-esteem and assertiveness!

OUTCOMES

By following these guidelines you should be able to feel more comfortable in looking at belief systems. However, if you feel that perhaps this is a little more in depth than you as a manager would like to go, you may find it more appropriate to enlist the help of your occupational health department or employee assistance programme (EAP) providers. If you work for a small organization it would be worth considering outsourcing to skilled professionals such as psychologists and counsellors.

You will find Tool 18 (Confidence Boosters) and Tool 19 (Harnessing Emotional Intelligence) particularly relevant to use alongside this tool.

TOOL 18: CONFIDENCE BOOSTERS

PURPOSE

There are times when we don't have the faith we should have in our ability to handle situations. We are either reluctant to try things out, or we believe (often mistakenly) that we haven't the skills to do it. This makes us lack confidence. Using these tools can improve confidence and self-esteem.

SITUATION

Lack of confidence in ourselves and low self-esteem often go together. If we aren't confident individuals we may well behave passively – anything for a quiet life, or aggressively – as a cover up for our own feelings of inadequacy.

Confidence boosters can be learned by anyone who fits in to either category. If people feel good about themselves, they will behave in a much more confident and assertive manner. As a manager, you may have identified specific individuals through the use of the questionnaires in this toolkit, who would particularly benefit from using these techniques as part of training and development courses.

DESCRIPTION

The three confidence boosters outlined here are:

- positive affirmations
- redirecting thinking
- challenging negative thoughts.

Each of these techniques will enable people to feel better about themselves.

METHOD

These exercises can be done by individuals on their own, a manager and employee together, or as part of a learning workshop focusing on personal development.

Positive affirmations

The British as a race of people are not very good at either telling themselves or others what they are good at. Some other nationalities find this easier, but if individuals are by nature rather shy and reserved they will find this exercise quite difficult.

Stand in front of a mirror and look directly at yourself. Say something nice about yourself:

- It may be a physical attribute:
  - I've got nice hair.
  - I have a good physique.
  - I've got a lovely smile.
- It may be a personality trait:
  - I have a sunny disposition.
  - I am a logical thinker.
  - I am kind and caring.
- It may be a skill:
  - I'm good at football.
  - I am a good negotiator.
  - I bake excellent cakes.

What does this feel like? Do you feel silly, and if so why? Are these things untrue? If they're not, why do you feel awkward?

Don't be tempted to compare yourself with other people. If you think that others are better than you, you will actually undermine yourself. What you are actually saying is 'I am worthless' and this will make you feel bad about yourself. Remind yourself that you are special, you are unique.

- Try to get over feeling silly, persevere and believe in yourself.
- When you have got used to telling yourself what you are good at and you have started to 'buy into' the idea then you can move on.
- Think of a situation you find hard to handle and begin to tell yourself you can cope. For example:

    'I can put forward my opinions on the new project.'

    'I can speak to Miss Hyde without feeling scared.'

    'I will tackle Jonathan about his timekeeping.'

The more you do this, the easier it will become.

Redirecting thinking

Quite often unwelcome thoughts pop into our head and undermine our confidence. This usually happens at the most inconvenient time and can make us fret or worry. If you follow these steps then there is a good chance that *you* will be in control (and not your thoughts)!

- If you are prone to worrying or ruminating on what might happen, then set a time aside each day to worry.
- Select a time of day when it is not going to interfere with anything else, for example, travelling home on the train, when you get home before your evening meal.
- Set time limits on this. Half an hour is usually more than enough. Be strict with yourself. If you haven't covered all your worries leave them until the next day.
- When intrusive thoughts occur during the day tell yourself that you will deal with them later. You are not procrastinating, you are merely redirecting your thoughts to a more convenient time.
- You may not come up with any solutions during this worry time – in fact it would be surprising if you did. This is not the object. The purpose of this exercise is to contain intrusive thoughts.

- When you redirect your thoughts to this specific time it will free you up to focus on more productive thinking.
- This will increase your confidence.

Challenging negative thoughts

When we lack confidence in ourselves we tend to focus on negative thinking. We assume that if things can go wrong, they probably will. If by nature we have a pessimistic outlook on life – that our cup is half empty rather than half full – this type of thinking is exacerbated. We need to break this cycle by turning our negative thinking into positive.

How do we do this?

Our inner dialogue (the conversations we have inside our head) may go along these lines:

> 'I'm really going to mess up this presentation.'
>
> 'I can't do this, it's too difficult.'
>
> 'I'm useless at driving, I'll never pass my test.'

This negative thinking saps our energy and debilitates us, preventing us from getting on with things.

When you have a negative thought, challenge it. Where is the evidence for that statement, can you back it up?

Taking an example from above:

> 'I'm useless at driving, I'll never pass my test.'

- Challenge: What evidence do I have to substantiate that statement?
  Let me think through the lessons I've had:
  - Have they all been hopeless?
  - When have I driven well?
  - How far have I progressed?
  - Does my instructor hold this view?
  … and so on.

By challenging negative thinking you can move towards a positive interpretation of the situation.

- Positive:
  - I did a good three point turn last week.
  - I'm much better at dealing with roundabouts than I used to be.
  - I don't get as flustered in busy traffic.
  - If I concentrate I can do well.

There are lots of other situations that you can tackle in this way, it just takes practice.

OUTCOMES

Looking at things from a different perspective helps to improve confidence. There is always more than one interpretation of a situation, and if we look for it we will find that we develop an upward positive spiral, rather than a downward negative one. Use these techniques in conjunction with Tool 17: Challenging and Changing Thinking. This will help to dispel the negative and unproductive beliefs people hold about themselves.

TOOL 19: HARNESSING EMOTIONAL INTELLIGENCE

Emotional intelligence is a relatively new concept developed by (amongst others) psychologist Daniel Goleman. Most of us are familiar with the notion of IQ (intelligence quotient) but not EQ (emotional quotient).

Goleman suggests that EQ is vital to us, not only in our everyday lives but in our work, and that those individuals who possess a high EQ are more likely to succeed in business and have more fulfilling personal and work relationships.

PURPOSE

The concept of emotional intelligence is included here for two reasons. The first is that it synthesizes the competencies we need as human beings to understand ourselves and others. This gives us insight into how we can manage ourselves and interact with others more effectively. Secondly, there are techniques which can be learned, based on the concept of emotional intelligence, that will help to regulate behaviour and improve interpersonal skills.

SITUATION

Emotional intelligence is something which has relevance to all aspects of life. In a work sense it is particularly useful when working with individuals who find it difficult to control their emotions, cannot empathize with others and have poor social skills. In this sense the techniques described here will be particularly pertinent to both the victims and the perpetrators of bullying.

The tools in this section can be used by individuals, in one-to-one sessions between a manager and employee, or as part of training and development programmes. The self-assessment profiles can be used as part of the appraisal process or as an exercise to use in team building. The diary can be done privately by individuals, but is more powerful when discussed with someone. It could be used by a manager and employee, but equally a mentor or counsellor would find it useful as the basis for discussing changing behaviour and thinking. The exercises which are about building rapport with others can be used by individuals, but again they are helpful in one-to-one meetings or as part of a training programme aimed at improving communication.

DESCRIPTION

Goleman suggests that there are two elements to emotional intelligence:

1 Personal competence

This includes:

- self-awareness
- self-regulation.

2 Social competence.

Individuals who bully appear to have poor emotional intelligence. They are unaware that their behaviour causes offence or is unacceptable. They are not able to show restraint and manage their emotions and feelings appropriately. Their motivation may be self-oriented with little understanding and empathy towards the feelings of others, and they lack competent social skills.
Conversely, victims of bullying inadvertently perpetuate the problem by their lack of awareness of their own emotional state.

There are several ways in which the principles of emotional intelligence can be applied to the work situation. These are:

1 By keeping a diary which records thoughts, feelings and actions.
2 By showing empathy towards others which will help to develop rapport with colleagues.
3 By using a self-assessment profile based on personal/relationship competencies and leadership skills.

METHOD

The diary

This should be completed by the individual over a period of time. One or two weeks is usually sufficient to get some idea of what they are thinking and feeling.

An example of a behavioural diary can be found on pages 162–165.

Behavioural Diary Template

Trigger/event	Thinking	Feeling/emotion	Behaviour
Look at preceding events. What happens? Or what are you doing to arouse certain thoughts and emotions?	What is the self-talk that goes through your head? Is it fuelling the emotion? Is it positive or negative?	Think of the 4 emotions – fear, sadness, joy and anger. What are you feeling now? Can you rate it on a scale of 1–10 (1 being low and 10 being high)?	What do you actually do as a result of this process? Look at the connections between thought, feelings and behaviour.

Record your experiences

The first column of the behavioural diary (triggers or events) is about situations or people that cause problems. You will need to think through where you have difficulties, for example:

'My manager speaks critically to me about my work.'

'I have to go into the board meeting.'

'Mr Jones has a go at me about being off sick.'

'Janet pushes me to take on more work.'

You will need to identify specific situations, rather than generalities.

Once you have identified the trigger move onto the next section marked 'Thinking'. In this column write down what you are thinking, for example:

'I wish he would leave me alone.'

'I'm damned if she's going to get away with it.'

'I'm useless at this job.'

'I'm getting out of here, I can't stand this any more.'

Our thoughts drive our emotions (it also happens the other way round – think of that Monday morning feeling), and depending on what we are thinking our emotional state will be either positive, negative or neutral. What we think or say to ourselves in our heads is referred to as 'self-talk' or 'internal dialogue'. Our self-talk can be destructive or constructive, but if it is the former it usually leads to negative feelings and unproductive outcomes.

Once you have documented your self-talk, think about how this makes you feel (see third column marked Feeling/Emotion). Describe the emotion and rate its intensity, for example:

- Irritated 7
- Frustrated 8
- Upset 8

Finally, note down what you actually do as a result of this trigger, that is, what your actual behaviour is, for example:

- Walk out of the room.
- Stand dejectedly with your head in your hands.
- Launch into a verbal slanging match.
- Burst into tears.

Although this may sound time consuming, it will get easier if you persevere. The more 'evidence' or information you collect by keeping your diary, the more it will become apparent why you behave as you do. Tables 8.1 and 8.2 will help you see how it all hangs together.

This is only the first step in using the diary! For the next part it will help if you work with a friend or someone you trust. You need to work out alternatives.

There are two things you can do to behave in a more positive manner if you find yourself in a situation that you find hard to handle:

Table 8.1 Behavioural diary – example 1

Trigger/event	Thinking	Feeling/emotion	Behaviour
Miss Brown asks me to see her in her office at 09.30.	'Oh my God, what have I done wrong now?' 'She's going to give me a telling off.' 'She's a right old battleaxe, I'll never stand up to her.' 'What am I going to do if she fires me?'	Panic 10 Helplessness 8 Annoyance with self 9	Heart starts racing, dash to the toilet, feel sick, want to get away.

Table 8.2 Behavioural diary – example 2

Trigger/event	Thinking	Feeling/emotion	Behaviour
Barry makes a suggestive remark about my appearance and leers at me.	'He's such a creep, I loathe him.' 'He's my boss so what can I do?' 'He's so nice to everyone else, no one will believe me if I tell them what he's really like.' 'I'm going to look for another job, I can't take much more of this.'	Anger 8 Self-consciousness 7 Helplessness 8 Despair 7	Clam up and look away, when he leaves go to the ladies toilet and cry my eyes out.

- You can challenge your thinking.
- You can behave differently.

Look at the tools which are based on assertiveness training, confidence boosters, challenging and changing belief systems and relaxation techniques (Tools 11–14, 16–18 and 21).

These will help you to reframe your thinking and enable you to behave more confidently.

Let's reshape the examples given earlier, to produce a more effective outcome.

Example 1: Miss Brown

- **Triggers/events** – Miss Brown asks me to see her in her office at 09.30.
- **Thinking** – Initially this was unproductive, for example 'What have I done wrong?'

Let's re-frame this thinking based on evidence (see Table 8.3).

Thinking in a more positive way will lead to more positive emotions.

Behaviour – initially this was unproductive, that is, heart racing, dashing to the toilet, feeling sick, wanting to get away.

More positive behaviour would be to:

Table 8.3 Example 1 – revised

From	To
Oh my God, what have I done wrong?	My work has been fine recently, I can't think of any gaffes or mistakes.
She's going to give me a telling off.	Why should she? I have met my targets, worked well with clients and colleagues. I haven't done anything that she can tell me off about.
She's an old battleaxe, I'll never stand up to her.	It's true she can be very tough, she needs to be in some ways. However, if I remain calm, listen to her and focus on what I know I'll feel better.
What am I going to do if she fires me?	She has no reason to fire me, I'm getting things out of proportion.

1. Use relaxation techniques prior to the meeting (see Tool 21).
2. If appropriate, prepare a script beforehand.
3. Listen carefully to what is being said.
4. Respond in a way which meets your needs as well as theirs.

Example 2: Barry

- **Triggers/events** – Barry makes a suggestive remark about my appearance and leers at me.
- **Thinking** – Initially this was unproductive, for example helplessness: 'What can I do?'

Let's reframe this thinking to generate some more positive responses (see Table 8.4).

Re-framing your thinking like this will lead to a more confident and positive frame of mind. As this happens you will feel more in control and more able to change the situation.

Behaviour – initially this was unproductive and in a sense was perpetrating 'victim' mode.

More productive behaviour would be:

1. To stand your ground and let him know that you find his behaviour offensive and unacceptable.

Table 8.4 Example 2 – revised

From	To
He's such a creep, I loathe him.	His behaviour is unacceptable and I don't have to put up with it.
He's my boss, so what can I do?	Okay, he's my boss but that doesn't mean there is nothing I can do. I can either tackle this myself or speak to someone in personnel.
He's so nice to everyone else, no one will believe me if I tell them what he's really like.	I can keep a record of what he says and does, and how it makes me feel. I can use this to back up my side of things.
I'm going to look for another job, I can't take much more of this.	I like my job and I think it's wrong that I have to consider leaving because of him. I'm going to try and sort this out before I do something so extreme.

2 To use the Broken Record technique (Tool 13) to reinforce how you feel.
3 To use confident body posture and maintain eye contact.
4 To practise relaxation techniques to relieve tension after your encounter.

Outcomes

Keeping a diary in this way will enable you to see how events and triggers lead to thinking, feeling and behaviour. If your thinking is 'skewed' or negative, then it is likely that you will *feel* negative in some way and your behaviour will not be productive.

By tackling your thinking and behaviour in a constructive way (as described in the examples) you will gain control over your situation and your confidence will grow.

Empathy

Empathy is about having an awareness and understanding of the needs and feelings of others, and being able to see things from their perspective. People who use bullying tactics are obviously not very skilled in this department, but it is surprising how many managers and supervisors lack empathy. The good news is that it is very easy to improve your empathic abilities. It is about communicating with others and taking an interest in them. However, this must be done with honesty and sincerity and not in a manipulative way to achieve your own ends.

The methodology for improving empathy is simple. All you need to do is to notice and make the most of opportunities as they arise, for example when you pass a colleague's desk, on your coffee break or when you are discussing a piece of work. It is about making the effort.

For example:

1 Notice the value of your staff by:
- smiling, nodding and saying 'hello'
- passing the time of day with them
- knowing who they are and what they do in the organization.

2 Show your appreciation of your staff verbally by:
- saying 'thank you' when they carry out a task, or when something is done well
- commenting on specific pieces of work
- not always focusing on the negative – if something is wrong use the PNP (positive – negative – positive) approach:
  - P   Thanks very much for doing …
  - N   But there are a few things I want you to look at.
  - P   I'd appreciate it by …

3 Show interest in their personal lives by:
- remembering the names of children and partners
- being interested in their hobbies and leisure activities or where they went on holiday.

4 Listen to them:
- Use active listening skills.
- Try and imagine what things are like for them.
- How would you feel and cope in their situations? (Be careful not to come up with solutions or advice.)

Outcomes

If you practise these guidelines on a regular basis (and it only takes a few minutes at a time), you will start to build up a rapport with colleagues and improve your working relationships.

RELATIONSHIP AND LEADERSHIP PROFILES

The two profiles on pages 168–169 examine the traits which are perceived as being important in developing and sustaining good interpersonal relationships and in possessing good leadership skills. The profiles are bipolar opposites, for example:

- fair and unfair
- warm and cold
- objective and subjective.

For each profile, the desirable traits are listed down the left hand side, with undesirable traits on the right hand side. Ask individuals to complete the profile and circle which score most suits them. You can complete the profile yourself and circle which score most suits you. So, for example, if they were rating themselves on loyalty as a desirable trait, they may feel that they are always loyal come what may. In which case they would circle (5). If, on the other hand, they feel that they are certainly loyal to friends and family, but not always to their employer, they might circle (3) – and so on.

You can also ask someone else to rate how they see you. Getting other people's perceptions of you can be very enlightening and can stimulate discussion and debate.

If you are working with someone who tends to use bullying tactics, these profiles can be revealing. If they see themselves as being 'open, empathic and accepting', but the evidence is to the contrary, then they obviously have a very different view of themselves than others do. If this is the case you will need to ask them (in a sensitive manner) why they consider themselves to be open, and so on. Ask them to give examples to support their thinking, and if they fudge or get annoyed then you will need to be able to provide examples yourself to illustrate your point.

You need to be able to challenge their views, but in a way which is non-confrontational.

OUTCOMES

Once you have identified certain traits that could be improved or developed you can help the individual to put together an Action Plan (Tool 20) which is specifically relevant to them.

Relationship Profile

Name _____

(Please circle the number which you feel most describes you)

FAIR	5	4	3	2	1	0	1	2	3	4	5	UNFAIR
CONSISTENT	5	4	3	2	1	0	1	2	3	4	5	INCONSISTENT
LOYAL	5	4	3	2	1	0	1	2	3	4	5	DISLOYAL
HONEST	5	4	3	2	1	0	1	2	3	4	5	DISHONEST
SENSE OF HUMOUR	5	4	3	2	1	0	1	2	3	4	5	HUMOURLESS
WARM	5	4	3	2	1	0	1	2	3	4	5	COLD
SYMPATHETIC	5	4	3	2	1	0	1	2	3	4	5	UNSYMPATHETIC
OPEN	5	4	3	2	1	0	1	2	3	4	5	CLOSED
EMPATHIC	5	4	3	2	1	0	1	2	3	4	5	NOT EMPATHIC
ACCEPTING	5	4	3	2	1	0	1	2	3	4	5	CRITICAL
NON-JUDGEMENTAL	5	4	3	2	1	0	1	2	3	4	5	JUDGEMENTAL

Leadership Profile

Page 1 of 3

Name _____

(Please circle the number which you feel most describes you)

COMMITTED	5	4	3	2	1	0	1	2	3	4	5	NON-COMMITTED
OBJECTIVE	5	4	3	2	1	0	1	2	3	4	5	SUBJECTIVE
ARTICULATE	5	4	3	2	1	0	1	2	3	4	5	INARTICULATE
FORCEFUL	5	4	3	2	1	0	1	2	3	4	5	INDECISIVE
PERSUASIVE	5	4	3	2	1	0	1	2	3	4	5	NOT PERSUASIVE
INNOVATIVE/CREATIVE	5	4	3	2	1	0	1	2	3	4	5	UNIMAGINATIVE
BRING CLARITY TO ISSUES	5	4	3	2	1	0	1	2	3	4	5	FUDGE ISSUES
TEAM BUILDER	5	4	3	2	1	0	1	2	3	4	5	LONER
FACILITATE DISCUSSION/DEBATE	5	4	3	2	1	0	1	2	3	4	5	IMPOSE OWN VIEWS
PROBLEM SOLVER	5	4	3	2	1	0	1	2	3	4	5	NOT A PROBLEM SOLVER
KEEP BALANCE BETWEEN PEOPLE AND TASKS	5	4	3	2	1	0	1	2	3	4	5	OPT FOR TASKS

Page 2 of 3

Is the problem **Sorted?** ☐ Yes ☐ No

Well on its way? ☐ Yes ☐ No

Needs some more work? ☐ Yes ☐ No

Next stage

a) If the problem has been resolved then no further action needs to be taken.

b) If it is on its way but still needs some work, then continue with the strategy for an agreed time (for example, 2 weeks). Set a review date. ....

c) If the strategy is not successful it may need an overhaul. Move on to this four stage plan:

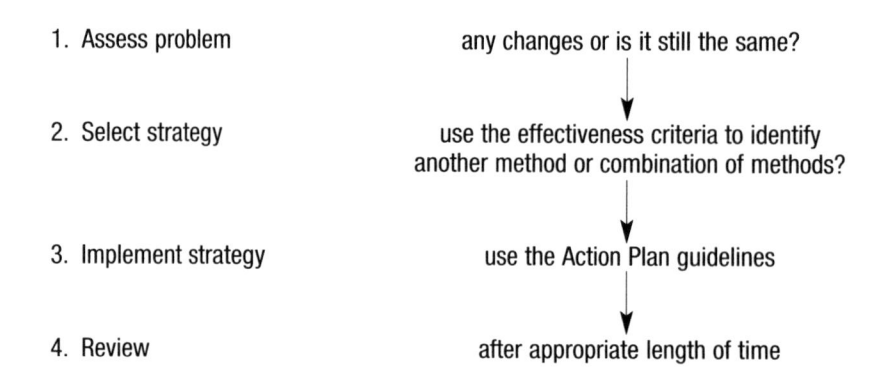

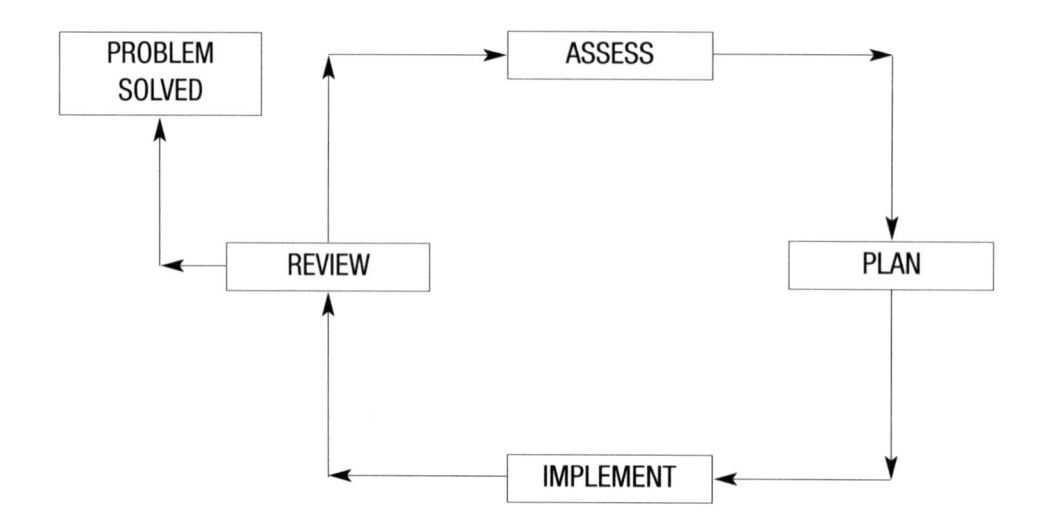

1. Assess problem	any changes or is it still the same?
2. Select strategy	use the effectiveness criteria to identify another method or combination of methods?
3. Implement strategy	use the Action Plan guidelines
4. Review	after appropriate length of time

PROBLEM SOLVED → ASSESS → PLAN → IMPLEMENT → REVIEW → (PROBLEM SOLVED)

Page 3 of 3

New strategy

_____
_____
_____
_____

When will I put this into place?

_____
_____

When will I review the problem? (Be realistic in your timeframe, for example, 1–2 weeks, to maintain impetus.)

_____
_____

Reviewing the problem

How many times have I used this strategy? ☐

Brief notes on what happened

_____
_____
_____

Degree of effectiveness: (on a scale 0 to 10)

Occasion 1

| 0 | 5 | 10 |

Occasion 2

| 0 | 5 | 10 |

Occasion 3

| 0 | 5 | 10 |

Occasion 4

| 0 | 5 | 10 |

How do I feel about this?

_____
_____

TOOL 20: MAKING AN ACTION PLAN

PURPOSE

To put things into action it is best to draw up a plan which enables you to do things in a systematic and logical way. It helps to be clear about the problem, which strategies are effective (and which may not be), when things will be reviewed, and how you feel about the process.

SITUATION

The action plan can be used by individuals once their problem has been defined and a strategy for putting it right has been selected. It will help individuals to focus specifically on what they have to do to change their behaviour.

DESCRIPTION

The action plan asks the individual to set out very clearly what the problem is and how they usually react. It asks them to rate the effectiveness of their current strategy and how they feel about this. It asks individuals to identify a new strategy (using the many options available in the toolkit) and when it will be put into place. The action plan then asks the individual to review what has happened and how effective the new strategy has been, with guidelines as to how to move on if the strategy hasn't been totally successful.

Together with the action plan there is a set of criteria which check the effectiveness of the plan.

METHOD

The action plan contains rating scales which are used to monitor effectiveness and progress. However, it is easy to be subjective and make an arbitrary judgement. This is where the effectiveness criteria come in. They look at whether behaviour has changed for the better, and enable the changes to be analysed more critically and objectively.

The action plan can be completed by an individual on their own, or with help from a supervisor or manager. When it comes to reviewing the problem individuals will need to look at the ten criteria for effectiveness. They need to think about each occasion when they have used their new strategy. They should go through the ten points and decide whether they were able to achieve each of the criteria. If they tick all ten, then they can safely say it was a resounding success. Eight out of ten shows it is working well and five or six suggests that they are making progress but there is a little way to go. If they only score two or three, then perhaps they need to review their strategy to discover why it isn't working.

Individuals should look at the final stage of the action plan to help them decide what they need to do next. They may need to adjust what they are doing, or select another strategy. At this point it is useful to discuss where they are up to with their supervisor/manager, or a trusted colleague, who may be able to generate some ideas, especially if they are feeling a little despondent that things are not going as well as they would like.

On the other hand, if they are beginning to get to grips with the problem they should be feeling more competent and confident. If this is the case individuals need to ensure that they maintain their behaviour change, as the more they practise it, the more skilled they will become.

📄 Action Plan

This is a tool for use with anyone who is having difficulty coping with difficult behaviour in others.

N.B. You can only change the behaviour of others by changing your own behaviour.

Defining the problem(s):   (be specific not general)
For example, '*I find it difficult to deal with my boss when she shouts and bawls at me, especially when I'm doing my best to cope with a busy office.*'

How I usually react:

_____

_____

_____

Degree of effectiveness: (on a scale 0 to 10)

0 — 5 — 10

How do I feel about this?

_____

_____

_____

_____

REPRODUCED FROM *BULLYING IN THE WORKPLACE*, ELAINE DOUGLAS, GOWER, ALDERSHOT

📄 Effectiveness Criteria

	Tick if appropriate
1 You have resisted the temptation to do anything for a quiet life.	☐
2 You have been able to put across your point of view in an assertive, non-confrontational way.	☐
3 You have been able to acknowledge the other party's views, needs and opinions.	☐
4 You have managed to stay calm (at least on the surface).	☐
5 You have not lost your temper, felt weepy or broken down.	☐
6 You have tackled the situation and not avoided it.	☐
7 You have not withdrawn from or avoided the confrontation.	☐
8 You have felt more in control of your responses.	☐
9 You were able to reach agreement, either through compromise or a joint solution.	☐
10 You came away from the interaction feeling that you had achieved what you wanted to achieve.	☐

OUTCOMES

By using the action plan you will be able to see very clearly whether or not your strategy is working. You should stick with a strategy for at least a month before you decide if it is being effective. It takes time to change behaviour and you need to persevere. However, if you really feel that you are trying to do something which is not for you, and that you will never be able to master it, it is better to select another strategy from the toolkit, and try that instead.

TOOL 21: RELAXATION TECHNIQUES

PURPOSE

Whenever we have to deal with difficult people or confrontational situations it takes its toll on our well-being. There are some individuals who appear to be unaffected by conflict and unpleasantness, but they may have high blood pressure, suffer from IBS (Irritable Bowel Syndrome) or be permanently tetchy and bad-tempered. They may not make the connection, but it is there.

There are others who are even more sensitive to disagreements and conflict. These people may find that this sort of thing causes and creates a lot of stress. They do not like confrontation and tend not to manage the situation very well – which in turn often creates more problems.

Relaxation techniques are useful tools to help alleviate stress. Even if people feel that they are coping well, they help us to unwind by reducing the tension in our bodies.

SITUATION

These exercises can be done both at home and at the office as they only take a few minutes. The breathing technique is particularly useful if you are preparing for a meeting with someone or going into what you anticipate will be a difficult situation. The visualization exercise and relaxing muscles are best done somewhere where it is quiet and preferably private, although it is possible to do them at your desk and gain some benefit from them.

DESCRIPTION

All three exercises are about focusing attention away from the immediate environment. When breathing slowly, focus and concentrate on the air going in through your nostrils and out through your mouth. During visualization you need to create vivid imagery that harnesses as many senses as you can and when relaxing muscles you need to be aware of the tension and relaxation of each muscle group.

METHOD

Find somewhere quiet and private if at all possible. It helps to close your eyes when doing all three exercises as this will aid concentration. Each exercise will only last for a few minutes at a time. Once you have completed the exercises, don't jump up and dash off to do something else. Open your eyes and take a few minutes to reorientate yourself before resuming work.

Slow breathing

Breathe in through the nose and out through the mouth to a count of 10 each way. This slows down the heart rate and reduces the amount of adrenaline pumping round the body. Practise this for a minute or two. Be aware of your body slowing down.

Visualization

Take a few minutes to practise this. Sit comfortably and close your eyes. Let your mind wander through a place where you feel at ease or relaxed. This may be taking a walk by a river – imagine the water lapping and the birds singing. Try to imagine all your senses being involved. Visualize colours, sounds, smells and textures. Focus on the whole experience and try to keep any unwanted, obtrusive thoughts at bay by saying to yourself *'I will deal with that later.'*

Relaxing muscles

Find yourself a comfortable chair or somewhere you can lie down. Start with your feet. Tense your muscles for a few seconds and then relax them. Work your way up your body tensing and relaxing each muscle group. Concentrate on each set of muscles as you go along. Finally, tense and relax your facial muscles. You will need to do this part in private otherwise your colleagues may well wonder what is wrong with you!

There are many commercial tapes available which may help you to relax. Some people enjoy listening to music, while others prefer a soothing voice. It is a matter of choice and you may need to experiment to find out what suits you best.

OUTCOMES

These three techniques have been included because they take up little time and are effective in the work situation. They will give you some respite and help you to cope with the build up of stress during the working day. However, you may well need more than this. If stress is a major problem then you need to consider:

- Is your lifestyle contributing to the problem?
- Do you have a balanced diet?
- Do you get enough exercise?
- Do you minimize your smoking and/or drinking?
- Do you have hobbies and leisure activities so that you can switch off?
- Do you sleep well?
- Do you schedule time for rest (and NOT just flop exhausted in front of the television)?

If you answered 'no' to any of the above questions, then perhaps you need to think seriously about your lifestyle. As human beings we have fundamental needs which must be met for us to function properly. For example, if our diet or our sleep patterns are poor, we will not be equipped to deal with life as well as we might. If you consider that any of the above is a problem for you, then think about what changes you need to make to improve your lifestyle. Remember that if your body is in good shape, your mind will be too.

TOOL 22: MAKING A BUDDY

PURPOSE

Some staff are more vulnerable than others. They may be young or inexperienced or perhaps quite quiet and shy. What they need is support and encouragement, otherwise they may well flounder. This is not good news either for them or the organization. Using a buddy system can give the support and encouragement needed and can help individuals who find it difficult to assert themselves without some level of support.

SITUATION

You can introduce a buddy system into an organization on a number of levels:

- For new staff (say possibly during their probationary period).
- For staff experiencing problems at work.
- For staff who are returning to work after a long period of sickness absence.
- For staff who have disclosed that they have been bullied and have requested a befriender (buddy).

DESCRIPTION

A 'buddy' is usually an experienced member of staff but not necessarily someone in a senior role (in fact it usually works better if this is not the case). He or she would need to have a genuine interest in people and want to help – without being too pushy and interfering. The relationship between the buddy and the member of staff is informal and casual and should not be of the 'expert/novice' ilk.

METHOD

There are a number of things which need to be done before you launch a buddy system:

- Decide how many buddies you would need. This will depend on the size of the organization and you may need someone for each department. If it is a smaller company you may need one person who is prepared to work with people throughout the company.

- You may have individuals in mind, or you may prefer to send out a memo to see whether anyone is interested. If you do this, however, you will need to give some thoughts as to whom you select. This could be done by identifying certain crucial criteria that you feel are needed for the role and interviewing prospective candidates to see whether they match up.

- Once you have selected your buddies they will need briefing as to what the role entails. This will include:

- having an understanding of the company and how everything fits together
- (possibly) specific job knowledge
- helping newcomers fit into the company
- providing support when things are difficult
- acting as a confidante if necessary
- being professional and respecting confidentiality
- having excellent listening skills.

Once all this is in place the system can run. In a sense the buddy and the individual need to work out what level of contact suits them and where they will meet. For example, in the early stages it may be that they meet up every day for a coffee and a chat or a quick few words at the end of the day. This level of support may then pan out to once a week, perhaps for a more in-depth discussion. It will very much depend on the circumstances.

This case study illustrates how a buddy system might work.

Case study

Mandy is 19 years old and is relatively new to the company. She is a good worker, but is rather quiet and finds it hard to mix with the other young people in the busy office. Her supervisor Brenda picks up on the fact that Mandy seems to spend her break times sitting apart from the others, and looks rather lost and lonely.

She speaks to Mandy who gets rather tearful and tells Brenda that some of the other girls make fun of her because she doesn't go to the same pubs or clubs that they do. She explains that her parents are very strict and it is hard for her to go against their wishes. Brenda asks Mandy if she would like to use the buddy system they have in place. At first she is reluctant but agrees to give it a try.

Natalie is a few years older than Mandy, but has worked for the company for five years and knows most of the staff very well. She is outgoing and friendly and starts to spend some time with Mandy. They meet at lunchtime quite regularly and Mandy begins to open up to Natalie about what is going on at work and at home.

Natalie realizes that the other girls in the office are not being deliberately cruel, but see Mandy as being different and not fitting in. She has a quiet word with one or two of them, while at the same time helping Mandy to build up her confidence by encouraging her to approach the girls and engage in conversation.

Before too long she is accepted by them and they start to arrange lunchtime shopping expeditions. Natalie reduces her contact, but doesn't withdraw completely, letting Mandy know she's there if she needs her.

OUTCOMES

Encouraging a buddy system in an organization can have many benefits. Problems can be pre-empted and dealt with before they become major issues, and the tension and heat can be taken out of more difficult scenarios. It can also help individuals to feel as though they belong and that people care about them.

Further reading and useful contacts

BULLYING

Books

Adams, A. (1992), *Bullying at Work – How to Confront and Overcome it*, Virago.

Field, T. (1996), *Bully in Sight*, Success Unlimited.

Ishmael, I. (1999), *Bullying and Violence at Work*, Industrial Society.

Stephens, T. (1999), *Bullying and Sexual Harassment*, IPD Good Practice Series.

Articles

Finn, W. (1996), 'Outing the Bullies', *Human Resources*, Jan/Feb.

Luzio-Locket, A. (1995), 'Enhancing Relationships within Organisations: An Examination of a Practical Approach to Bullying at Work', *Employee Counselling Today*, 7(1).

Martin, N. (1997), 'Adult Workplace Bullying', *The Psychologist*, **10**(8).

Reports

UMIST (2000), *Destructive Interpersonal Conflict and Bullying at Work: Key Findings*.

Policy documents

The following documents can be obtained from the library of the Chartered Institute of Personnel and Development.

City of Liverpool (1995), *Harassment, Discrimination and Bullying Policy.*

Littlewoods (1996), *Promoting Employees' Dignity at Work.*

Nationwide (1996), *Harassment/Bullying Policy.*

Stoke Mandeville Hospital Trust (1997), *Policy on Harassment.*

Trade union guides

MSF (1995), *Bullying at Work: How to Tackle it. A Guide for MSF Representatives and Members.* Can be obtained from: MSF Health and Safety Office, Whitehall College, Dane O'Coys Road, Bishop Stortford, Herts CM23 2JN.

NASUWT (1996), *No Place to Hide – Confronting Workplace Bullies.* Can be obtained from: NASUWT, Hillscourt Education Centre, Rednal, Birmingham B45 8RS. Tel: 0121 453 6150.

Employment law

Pinsent Curtis, *Dignity at Work – The Law on Harassment and Bullying within the Workplace.* Can be obtained from: Pinsent Curtis (Law Firm), 41 Park Square, Leeds LS1 2NS. Tel: 0113 244 5000.

Useful contacts

Andrea Adams Trust
Maintime House
Basin Road North
Hove
East Sussex
BN41 1WA
Tel/Fax: 01273 417850

Elaine Douglas Associates Limited
EDA House
25 Hope Street
Douglas
Isle of Man
IM1 1AR
Tel: 01624 629264

Health and Safety Executive
HSE Information Centre
Broad Lane
Sheffield
S3 7HQ
Tel: 0114 289 2345

Industrial Society
Robert Hyde House
48 Bryanston Square
London
W1H 7LN
Tel: 020 7479 2000

Chartered Institute of Personnel and Development
CIPD House
Camp Road
London
SW19 4UX
Tel: 020 8971 9000

Suzy Lamplugh Trust
Training Department
PO Box 17818
London
SW14 8WW
Tel: 020 8876 0305

ADDITIONAL RESOURCES

Berne, E. (1968), *Games People Play*, Penguin.

Black, K. and Black, K. (1991), *Assertiveness at Work*, McGraw Hill.

Carlson, R. (1998), *Don't Sweat the Small Stuff*, Hodder and Stoughton.

Field, L. (1997), *60 Tips for Self-esteem*, Element.

Goleman, D. (1996), *Emotional Intelligence*, Bloomsbury Publishing.

Hopson, B., Scally M. and Stafford, K. (1992), *Transitions, the Challenge of Change*, Lifeskills Communications Limited.

Mulligan, E. (1997), *Life Coaching, Change your Life in 7 Days*, BCA.

Parsloe, E. (1999), *The Manager as Coach and Mentor*, IPD Management Series.

Sanders, P. (1998), *First Steps in Counselling*, PCCS Books.

Thomas, K.W. and Kilmann, R.H. (1974), *Thomas-Kilmann Conflict Mode Instrument*, Consulting Psychologists Press Inc.

Thorne, B. (1996) 'Person-Centred Therapy' in W. Dryden (ed.) *The Handbook of Individual Therapy*, Sage. (This chapter provides a good summary of Carl Rogers' work.)